Landmark Supreme Court Cases

THE UNITED STATES *v.* NIXON

THE WATERGATE SCANDAL AND LIMITS TO US PRESIDENTIAL POWER

by Erika Wittekind

Content Consultant
Michael Gerhardt
Samuel Ashe Distinguished Professor in Constitutional Law & Director,
Center for Law and Government, University of North Carolina at Chapel Hill

CREDITS

Published by ABDO Publishing Company, PO Box 398166, Minneapolis, MN 55439. Copyright © 2013 by Abdo Consulting Group, Inc. International copyrights reserved in all countries. No part of this book may be reproduced in any form without written permission from the publisher. The Essential Library™ is a trademark and logo of ABDO Publishing Company.

Printed in the United States of America,
North Mankato, Minnesota
062012
092012

 THIS BOOK CONTAINS AT LEAST 10% RECYCLED MATERIALS.

Editor: Lauren Coss
Series Designer: Emily Love

Library of Congress Cataloging-in-Publication Data
Wittekind, Erika, 1980-
  The United States v. Nixon : the Watergate scandal and limits to US presidential power / by Erika Wittekind ; content consultant: Michael J Gerhardt.
    p. cm. -- (Landmark Supreme Court cases)
  Includes bibliographical references.
  ISBN 978-1-61783-478-3
  1. United States--Trials, litigation, etc.--Juvenile literature. 2. Nixon, Richard M. (Richard Milhous), 1913-1994--Trials, litigation, etc.--Juvenile literature. 3. Executive privilege (Government information)--United States--Juvenile literature. 4. Watergate Affair, 1972-1974--Juvenile literature. 5. Trial and arbitral proceedings I. Gerhardt, Michael J., 1956- II. Title. III. Title: The United States vs. Nixon. IV. Title: The United States versus Nixon.
  KF228.U5W58 2013
  342.73'062--dc23

                                2012001281

Photo Credits

Rolls Press/Popperfoto/Getty Images, cover; AP Images, 9, 37, 39, 36, 52, 57, 65, 73, 84, 93, 126; Keystone/Getty Images, 18; North Wind/North Wind Picture Archives, 25; Victorian Traditions/Shutterstock Images, 26; Rembrandt Peale/AP Images, 30; Bettmann/Corbis/AP Images, 62, 97, 104, 107; John Duricka/AP Images, 80; Henry Griffin/AP Images, 3, 82; UPI/AP Images, 111; National Archives/AP Images, 117; Hulton Archive/Getty Images, 120; Nick Ut/ AP Images, 131; J. Scott Applewhite/AP Images, 134

Table of Contents

WHAT IS THE US SUPREME COURT?

The US Supreme Court, located in Washington DC, is the highest court in the United States and authorized to exist by the US Constitution. It consists of a chief justice and eight associate justices nominated by the president of the United States and approved by the US Senate. The justices are appointed to serve for life. A term of the court is from the first Monday in October to the first Monday in October the following year.

Each year, the justices are asked to consider more than 7,000 cases. They vote on which petitions they will grant. Four of the nine justices must vote in favor of granting a petition before a case moves forward. Currently, the justices decide between 100 and 150 cases per term.

The justices generally choose cases that address questions of state or federal laws or other constitutional questions they have not previously ruled on. The Supreme Court cannot simply declare a law unconstitutional; it must wait until someone appeals a lower court's ruling on the law.

HOW DOES THE APPEALS PROCESS WORK?

A case usually begins in a local court. For a case involving a federal law, this is usually a federal district court. For a case involving a state or local law, this is a local trial court.

If a defendant is found guilty in a criminal trial and believes the trial court made an error, that person may appeal the case to a higher court. The defendant, now called an appellant, files a brief that explains the error the trial court allegedly made and asks for the decision to be reversed.

An appellate court, or court of appeals, reviews the records of the lower court but does not look at other evidence or call witnesses. If the appeals court finds no errors were made, the appellant may

go one step further and petition the US Supreme Court to review the case. A case ruled on in a state's highest court may be appealed to the US Supreme Court.

A Supreme Court decision is based on a majority vote. Occasionally one or more justices will abstain from a case, however, a majority vote by the remaining justices is still needed to overturn a lower-court ruling. What the US Supreme Court decides is final; there is no other court to which a person can appeal. In addition, these rulings set precedent for future rulings. Unless the circumstances are greatly changed, the Supreme Court makes rulings that are consistent with its past decisions. Only an amendment to the US Constitution can overturn a Supreme Court ruling.

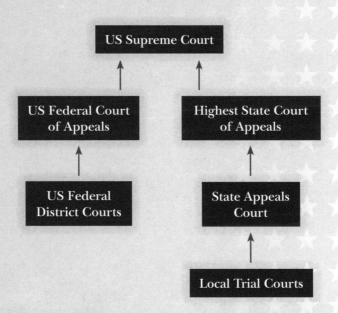

Chapter 1

Straight to the Supreme Court

*I*n his State of the Union address on January 30, 1974, President Richard Nixon announced to the US Congress that his office would be providing no more evidence for the ongoing investigation into the Watergate burglaries of the previous year. He claimed he had provided everything the **grand jury** needed to weigh the case, and he explained that further inquiry would distract from the nation's real concerns. "One year of Watergate is

> **grand jury**—A group of people selected to examine the charges against a suspect and determine if that suspect should be charged with a crime for which the suspect will be later tried.

By 1974, Richard Nixon's presidency was in jeopardy as a result of his role in the Watergate scandal.

enough," Nixon said.[1] This was news to Special Prosecutor Leon Jaworski, who had been appointed months earlier to continue the investigation into the president's alleged involvement in criminal activity and the ensuing cover-up.

A White House Scandal

The Watergate scandal began on June 17, 1972, when five men broke into the Democratic National Committee headquarters in Washington DC, which were located at an apartment and hotel complex known as the Watergate. The five burglars and two White House employees were charged with burglary and wiretapping. When five of the original **defendants** pleaded guilty and two were convicted by a jury, the matter appeared to have been put to rest. But a twist appeared when the judge announced the **sentence**. The judge read aloud a letter from one of the defendants suggesting involvement from high-ranking White House officials. The Senate launched its own investigation into the Watergate incident, which uncovered indications of Nixon's direct involvement. Congress approved the appointment of a special prosecutor to conduct an independent investigation of Nixon and his staff.

SPECIAL PROSECUTOR

In a criminal case regarding high-ranking government officials, someone is appointed to specifically lead the investigation of misconduct while in office. The purpose of the position is to prevent a conflict of interest between the Department of Justice and the investigated parties, who may have political ties to each other. At the time of Watergate, it was the job of the attorney general, who heads the Department of Justice, to appoint a special prosecutor and set guidelines designed to establish that person's independence. In 1978, following Watergate, Congress set more standard rules for the position, which then became known as independent prosecutor.

Over the next few years, Nixon faced a firestorm of criticism and calls for his **impeachment** after he had the investigation's original special prosecutor fired. Nixon agreed to turn over a handful of tapes of conversations held in the Oval Office. It was a small fraction of the materials requested by Jaworski and previous investigators. The fact that one of the released tapes contained an 18-and-a-half-minute gap, claimed to be

defendant—The person against whom legal action is brought.
impeachment—The charging of a public official with a crime.
sentence—A decision by a judge or court including the punishment for the person convicted.

caused by a recording error, heightened suspicions that Nixon had more to hide. The special prosecutor's office had already uncovered clues suggesting the wrongdoing of the White House far surpassed the Watergate burglary. The evidence pointed to Nixon's involvement in another break-in, interference in government agencies, and campaign-finance law violations. Evidence also supported the existence of the Plumbers, a group of White House staff members in charge of identifying and preventing information leaks. But the special prosecutor's office had not yet obtained solid proof of these connections.

RECORDED CONVERSATIONS

When Nixon arrived at the White House as president in 1969, he had the existing recording systems dismantled. In 1971, he changed his mind and decided to start recording conversations for record-keeping purposes. Between February 16, 1971, and July 18, 1973, Nixon recorded approximately 4,000 hours of meetings and phone conversations in the Oval Office and several other meeting rooms. The recording devices were activated by sound instead of manually, so at times conversations were recorded unintentionally.

The Power of Executive Privilege

When Jaworski checked on the status of his evidence requests following the president's State of the Union address, Nixon's criminal lawyer, James St. Clair, reminded Jaworski of the president's stance: the requested tapes and documents fell under Nixon's executive privilege. Executive privilege refers to the right of the **executive branch** of government to withhold documents and communications when their release would negatively affect an executive branch member's ability to govern. Nixon claimed Jaworski's requests did not justify overriding the executive privilege. He claimed that turning over the tapes would open the door to unlimited intrusions on the president's private deliberations. Through St. Clair, Nixon cited the separation of powers contained in the US Constitution as a basis for executive privilege. St. Clair wrote in his response to Jaworski:

> *From the beginning of the investigation of the Watergate affair, there has been a conflict between*

---

executive branch—One of three branches of the federal government; it is headed by the president and charged with implementing and enforcing laws.

two critical requirements: the need for a complete and thorough investigation; and the need to make sure that the investigation was handled in a way that the important **Constitutional** *boundaries between the branches of government were respected and retained.*[2]

The conflict stated by St. Clair foreshadowed the one that would soon be taken up by the US Supreme Court. When the grand jury handed down a new slew of Watergate **indictments** on March 1, 1974, with

A GRAND JURY TRIAL

A trial jury consists of between six and 12 members that hear evidence during a trial and deliver a verdict on the case. A grand jury, on the other hand, is made up of 16 to 23 members, and it meets before a trial. All federal felonies are heard before a grand jury unless the defendant waives his or her right to a grand jury trial. State courts may or may not use grand juries at their own discretion. The prosecutor presents evidence, after which the grand jury determines whether or not there is probable cause to charge the defendant with a crime. If there is a probable cause, it is likely enough that the accused committed the crime to warrant a full criminal trial. If enough evidence is presented to determine probable cause, the grand jury issues an indictment. Unlike trials, grand jury proceedings are not open to the public.

the president named as an unindicted coconspirator, Jaworski continued to push the White House for the evidence needed to go to trial. As special prosecutor, he sought to **subpoena** tapes and documents related to 64 conversations between Nixon and his top aides.

Judge John Sirica, chief judge for the US District Court for the District of Columbia, who was overseeing the Watergate hearings, granted the subpoena on April 16. However, Jaworski knew the president would not give in without a fight. The conflict seemed destined to reach the nation's highest court. St. Clair petitioned Sirica to stop the subpoena, but Sirica refused. St. Clair then **appealed** to the US **Court of Appeals** for the District of Columbia Circuit to overrule Sirica's decision and stop the subpoena.

appealed—Petitioned a higher court to review the decision or proceedings of a lower court.

constitutional—In accordance with a constitution.

court of appeals—A federal court that hears cases appealed from the district courts in its circuit.

indictment—A formal written statement by a prosecutor or grand jury officially charging someone with an offense.

subpoena—An order that commands a person to appear in court or to submit evidence.

A Race to the Supreme Court

Time was of the essence. The Supreme Court **justices** were scheduled to end their session on June 17. If a lower **appellate court** heard the case first, the trial was unlikely to make it to the Supreme Court before it broke for the summer, and a final decision on the subpoena would not arrive until fall. The Watergate trial for the indictments handed down by the grand jury was set to begin on September 9, 1974. Assuming the subpoena was upheld by the Supreme Court, the time needed to obtain and assess the evidence would have delayed the Watergate criminal trial until the spring of 1975. Jaworski felt it was important to the nation's well-being not to delay the criminal proceedings of Watergate any longer than necessary. He also feared the case would be delayed indefinitely and might never come to trial. With this in mind, Jaworski petitioned to bypass the appeal process and go directly to the Supreme Court.

A case can bypass the appeals process and be heard directly by the Supreme Court in cases of "imperative public importance as to require immediate settlement."[3] The court had only ever used this rule, rule 20, twice since World War II (1939–1945), once in 1947 in a case concerning the United Mine Workers Strike and again

when President Harry Truman took national control of steel mills during the Korean War (1950–1953).

To get his case heard by the Supreme Court, Jaworski had to file a petition for a **writ of certiorari**. In his petition, Jaworski asked the court to hear the case immediately so the evidence could be obtained and the trial could be conducted in a timely manner.

appellate court—A court that can review and reverse the judgment of a lower court.

justice—A member of the US Supreme Court.

writ of certiorari—An order from a higher court to a lower court calling for the record of a case for review.

Leon Jaworski served as special prosecutor in the
Watergate investigation.

He pointed out that the court of appeals had already
issued an opinion on the issue when it upheld subpoenas
by Archibald Cox, who was Jaworski's predecessor as
special prosecutor. Therefore, it seemed reasonable to
bypass that appeals step. His petition also laid out the
issues of the case. He asked the court to review five
points: whether the president had to comply with the
subpoenas; whether his claim of executive privilege
allowed him to withhold evidence in a criminal trial of

his own aides; whether confidentiality could be claimed concerning discussions of a criminal conspiracy and cover-up; whether the president had already waived his executive privilege by turning over some of the evidence; and whether the requested tapes and documents were relevant and could be used as evidence.

St. Clair submitted an opposing **brief** to the Supreme Court, arguing the full **judicial** process should be followed. The brief stated:

> *When a case raises the most fundamental issues of the allocation of power among the three branches of the federal government, it is more important that it be decided wisely than that it be decided hurriedly.*[5]

St. Clair also argued the criminal trial of individuals was not of enough national importance to bypass the appeals process.

A Controversial Case

The court's decision arrived on May 31, 1974, the day after St. Clair submitted his brief. The Supreme Court

brief—A document that establishes the legal argument of a case.
judicial—Relating to justice or the courts.

merely stated that the expedited writ for certiorari had been granted. Oral arguments in front of Supreme Court justices were scheduled for July 8. The court's decision surprised many legal minds and politicians who had believed the justices would be hesitant to disregard the usual appeals process in such a controversial case. Some thought the justices' decision was politically motivated. Nixon had appointed four of the justices. This case would be a test of whether their loyalty to Nixon was stronger than their commitment to the law. If the court had voted not to hear the case and to use the normal appeals process instead, the decision might have been perceived as aiding the president.

Justice William Brennan's notes on the decision were later released. The notes reveal that six justices were initially opposed to taking the case. Justice William Douglas argued the case should be heard by the court of appeals first. Justices Harry Blackmun and Potter Stewart did not see the harm in delaying the criminal trial concerning Watergate. Justice Byron White expressed misgivings about Jaworski's motives. Brennan, however, was in favor of taking the case and stated that if the court declined to take it, he would write a **dissenting** opinion. The court had a "duty to our institution and to the public not to delay," he argued.[6] Thurgood Marshall agreed with Brennan, and

after debating the issue, Powell, Stewart, Douglas, and **Chief Justice** Warren Burger joined them in voting to hear the case. Blackmun and White voted no on the grounds that the case did not meet the guidelines for an expedited writ of certiorari.

With that, the justices were set to hear arguments in a case that would determine a fundamental constitutional question: to what extent can the holder of the highest office in the country hold himself or herself above the law? It would be a case that would affect the scope and the power of the US presidency for years to come. ～

> [The Nixon administration was] the most scandal-ridden administration in American history. And those scandals did not involve merely the looting of the public treasury by public officials. . . . They revolved around a variety of illegal and extralegal political actions directed by the president and his chief assistants, including the former attorney general of the United States, that attempted to subvert the American political system."[7]
>
> —*MELVIN SMALL, NIXON BIOGRAPHER*

chief justice—The presiding judge of the US Supreme Court.

dissent—An official written statement of a Supreme Court justice who disagrees with the majority decision.

Chapter 2

The Historical Roots of Executive Privilege

Richard Nixon was not the first president to claim executive privilege. The term *executive privilege* was first used in 1958, when Supreme Court Justice Stanley F. Reed wrote it in an opinion, but the idea has been around for much longer.[1] Although the term does not appear in the US Constitution explicitly, those who claim the privilege exists have argued it is implied by the separation of powers. This refers to the division of powers among the three branches of the US government: executive, legislative, and judicial. For each branch, the constitutional

SEPARATION OF POWERS

The US Constitution divides power between the three branches of government. A system of checks and balances ensures no single branch of government has too much power. Each branch's powers are limited, or checked, by the other two branches. For example, when Congress passes a law, the president has the power to veto, or overrule, it, or the Supreme Court can rule the law unconstitutional.

framers defined and limited powers. A system of checks and balances prevents any one branch from assuming too much control.

Presidents who exert executive privilege have argued that the constitutional separation of powers means the legislative and judicial branches are limited in how much they can influence the activities of the executive branch. Presidents and their staff members might not feel they could speak or act freely knowing they might face investigation by the other branches of government. This might negatively affect the way they do their jobs, potentially putting the entire country in danger. Because it is not written into the Constitution or formalized in any other law, executive privilege is part of common law.

BRITISH INFLUENCE

Coming from an English background, the framers of the US Constitution considered the history of executive power in Great Britain while deciding how powerful to make the American chief executive. "For centuries, English law provided that 'the king can do no wrong,' and untold generations suffered the consequences of an unchecked monarchy," wrote one historian.[2] In 1215, the English rejected that principle with the Magna Carta, a document proclaiming English citizens' rights within a monarchy. These fundamental rights, which reject an infallible monarchy, can be seen in the US Constitution.

It has been established through following **precedents** set by the court system.

The concept of executive privilege was first debated during George Washington's presidency. In 1792, Congress asked to see documents concerning General Arthur St. Clair's failed 1791 military mission against Native American tribes in Ohio. Washington's cabinet debated whether to honor the request, advising the president he could withhold documents pertaining to activities of the executive branch if it was in the

precedent—A court ruling or decision that becomes an example and is noted in later rulings in similar cases.

The Magna Carta, signed in England in 1215, set the stage for limits to executive power.

President George Washington was the first US president and the first president to claim the principle of executive privilege.

public interest to do so. While Washington ended up giving Congress the documents concerning St. Clair's expedition, on several other occasions he denied similar requests based on his cabinet's recommendation. In 1796, Washington declined to comply with the US House of Representatives' request for materials regarding the Jay Treaty between the United States and Great Britain. Washington reasoned that because the House played no role in the ratification of treaties it did not have a pressing need to see the documents.

Judicial Review

How much power the **judicial branch** had in relation to the other two branches was not well established during the presidencies of Washington or his successor, John Adams. In the early days of the United States, the Supreme Court interpreted laws but did not declare laws **unconstitutional**. The Supreme Court established the power to declare laws unconstitutional in the 1803 case *Marbury v. Madison*. In this case, President

---

judicial branch—One of three branches of the federal government; it includes the nation's court system and decides if laws are constitutional.

unconstitutional—Inconsistent with a constitution.

Adams made a number of new judicial appointments just before leaving office in 1801. One of the new appointees, William Marbury, did not receive written notice of his appointment to justice of the peace due to an administrative error. Newly elected President Thomas Jefferson did not give Marbury the commission, even though the Senate had confirmed him. According to one historian, "In effect, Jefferson declared that he had the power to do what he pleased, and he dared Marbury to do something about it."[3] Marbury decided to sue Secretary of State James Madison over the matter. Under a provision of the Judiciary Act of 1789, which set up the organization

> " The judicial Power shall extend to all Cases, in Law and Equity, arising under this Constitution, the Laws of the United States, and Treaties made, or which shall be made, under their Authority;—to all Cases affecting Ambassadors, other public Ministers and Consuls;—to all Cases of admiralty and maritime Jurisdiction;—to Controversies to which the United States shall be a Party;—to Controversies between two or more States;—between a State and Citizens of another State,— between Citizens of different States,—between Citizens of the same State claiming Lands under Grants of different States, and between a State, or the Citizens thereof, and foreign States, Citizens or Subjects."[4]
>
> —ARTICLE III OF THE US CONSTITUTION, ALLOWING FOR THE CREATION OF THE SUPREME COURT

of the US court system, the case went directly to the Supreme Court.

The court agreed that Marbury should have received his appointment, but it did not force Madison to allow Marbury to assume the justice of the peace position. Supreme Court Chief Justice John Marshall wrote the opinion, which asserted that the section of the Judiciary Act of 1789 violated the US Constitution, and therefore the Supreme Court lacked **jurisdiction** to hear the case. Marshall wrote in the court's opinion that the US Constitution is the "original and supreme will" of the people and must be followed above all else.[5] It was the first time the Supreme Court exercised the power of judicial review, a power that established the judicial branch as being equal to the other two branches. Since then, the Supreme Court has used the power to review and decide to uphold or strike down a law on the basis of whether or not it is constitutional. After a law is stricken, the only way to reverse it is to amend the Constitution. Marshall also wrote in the opinion,

jurisdiction—The authority to govern or try cases; also refers to the territory under that authority.

As president, Jefferson refused to acknowledge a commission awarded by his predecessor.

By the Constitution of the United States, the President is invested with certain important political powers, in the exercise of which he is to use his own discretion, and is accountable only to his country in his political character and to his own conscience.[6]

While expanding the power of the judicial branch in *Marbury v. Madison*, the court also laid the foundation for recognizing executive privilege.

Early Debates on Executive Privilege

The issue of judicial power arose again during Jefferson's presidency. In 1807, Aaron Burr, who served as vice president during Jefferson's first term, was tried for treason. He was accused of plotting to invade Spanish territory with the goal of building an independent government. The case ended up in the Supreme Court in *United States v. Burr*. Burr's lawyer asked the court to subpoena letters between Jefferson and Burr that were thought to contain information that would help **acquit** Burr. The Supreme Court ruled that Jefferson did not have to give up the documents, but it held that

acquit—To free a criminal suspect from charges.

the judicial branch does have the power to make such requests of the executive branch. Justice John Marshall stated that the court should balance the need to protect national security against the right of the individual to have a fair trial. The case is often cited as a key precedent for executive privilege.

Other presidents have faced requests from Congress to provide information, and these often have not resulted in court cases. Prior to the Civil War, presidents usually complied with requests for information by Congress. However, presidents such as Andrew Jackson, John Tyler, James Polk, and Franklin Pierce occasionally withheld information demanded by Congress.

Executive Privilege in the Twentieth Century

In the first half of the twentieth century, the Supreme Court recognized limited privilege for the executive branch. The 1927 case of *McGrain v. Daugherty* concerned the investigation of the Teapot Dome Scandal, in which Secretary of the Interior Albert Fall was accused of secretly leasing federal land to oil companies. The Supreme Court confirmed that Congress did have the power to conduct investigations of the executive

ENFORCEMENT OF RULINGS

While Supreme Court rulings are final, barring a constitutional amendment, it has been pointed out that the judicial branch has "no army"—meaning it depends on the other branches of government to enforce its rulings.[8] For example, when the Supreme Court ruled that schools had to be desegregated in *Brown v. Board of Education*, US troops, part of the executive branch, helped make sure all schools followed the ruling. However, if the other branches of government did not support a Supreme Court decision and chose not to act on its behalf, there might be no way to enforce a ruling.

branch and to issue subpoenas as needed. The court's opinion stated:

> *Issuance of subpoenas . . . has long been held to be a legitimate use by Congress of its power to investigate. . . . Experience has taught that mere requests for . . . information often are unavailing.*[7]

In 1948, the Supreme Court shed light on situations in which the president might have the right to refuse such requests for information, such as material regarding military or national security issues. The case, *Chicago Southern Air Lines, Inc. v. Waterman Steamship Corporation*, concerned the awarding of foreign air-traffic routes to certain airlines. The court upheld

that the executive branch could withhold information pertaining to foreign policy or in cases where secrecy was necessary for national security.

The court elaborated on its stance regarding state secrets when it considered *United States v. Reynolds* in 1953. When three civilians were accidentally killed during the testing of secret military airplanes, their widows requested information on the accident to file a **lawsuit**. The Supreme Court decision upheld the privilege of the US Air Force to withhold the documents, but the opinion established guidelines for assessing such claims. Chief Justice Fred M. Vinson stated that claims of privilege should be assessed on a case-by-case basis. He wrote,

> *Where there is a strong showing of necessity, the claim of privilege should not be lightly accepted, but even the most compelling necessity cannot overcome the claim of privilege if the court is ultimately satisfied that military secrets are at stake.*[9]

However, the court did not have any proof when it accepted the government's assertion that concealing

lawsuit—Legal action brought against a party.

the accident report was in the interest of national security. When the report was eventually declassified in 2000, it showed the aircraft that had crashed had been insufficiently maintained, which could have helped the widows win their lawsuit, but it did not contain any other sensitive information.

Claims of executive privilege began increasing starting in 1954 under President Dwight D. Eisenhower. The continued insistence on such a privilege coincided with Nixon's tenure as Eisenhower's vice president, setting the stage for Nixon's Supreme Court showdown in the 1970s. ∼

Chapter 3

The Rise of Richard Nixon

R ichard Milhous Nixon was born in 1913 in Yorba Linda, California, to Frank Nixon, owner of a service station and general store, and Hannah Milhous Nixon. In his memoir, he wrote, "I was born in a house my father built."[1] Despite his humble roots, Nixon quickly rose to national prominence. After graduating from Duke University Law School in 1937, he practiced law for several years before enlisting in the US Navy in 1942 and serving in World War II.

When he entered politics, Nixon gained a reputation as someone who wanted to win at all costs. He was elected to the US House of Representatives

Nixon spent his childhood and teenage years in Southern California.

for the first time in 1946, defeating a popular five-term incumbent representing a district of California. Critics said he won by waging a smear campaign, but the surprising victory gave Nixon national recognition. From 1948 to 1950, he served on the House Un-American Activities Committee, which investigated people suspected of having Soviet Union or Communist ties during the Cold War era. Through his determined questioning of accused Soviet spy Alger Hiss during the committee's hearings, Nixon gained national prominence and established a reputation as an anticommunist.

Running for a US Senate seat against Helen Gahagan Douglas in 1950, Nixon once again was accused of winning through a smear campaign. At this time, negative campaigning was not as common or accepted as it is today. Nixon distributed fliers portraying Douglas as a Communist sympathizer. "Even pro-Nixon accounts of the campaign concede that the campaign was 'the most hateful' California had experienced in years," wrote one historian. "By whatever description, the Nixon-Douglas campaign became a new standard for measuring negative campaigning."[2] A Southern California newspaper started calling Nixon

Running with Eisenhower, *left*, Nixon, *right*, made divisive statements so Eisenhower could maintain a positive image.

"Tricky Dick," a nickname that stuck with him through the years.

Running on Eisenhower's Ticket

After six years in Congress, Nixon was chosen as Dwight Eisenhower's running mate in the 1952 presidential election. While Nixon heavily criticized the Democratic candidates, which consisted of presidential nominee Adlai Stevenson and running mate John Sparkman, Eisenhower, who had fought in both World War I (1914–1918) and World War II, maintained his clean image as a national war hero. Similarly, the Democrats focused their criticism on Nixon, questioning whether he was fit to assume the presidency if called upon. Stevenson said Nixon was waging a campaign of "innuendo and accusations aimed at sowing the seeds of doubt and mistrust."[3]

The discovery that Nixon's campaign had a fund of donations from California businessmen for his personal use stirred up controversy. Many other politicians operated similar funds, but Nixon's fund ran counter to Eisenhower's campaign pledge to clean up Washington. Instead of dropping Nixon outright, the Eisenhower campaign gave Nixon a chance to explain himself. Nixon counterattacked the accusations with a speech calling attention to Stevenson's own slush fund and other controversies surrounding the Democrats.

Most memorably, Nixon confessed to receiving one political gift he intended to keep— his dog, Checkers, whom his daughters adored. He implied that the Democrats would stoop so low as to deprive his family of a beloved pet. Some saw it as a

> " One other thing I probably should tell you, because if I don't they'll probably be saying this about me, too. We did get something, a gift, after the election. A man down in Texas heard Pat on the radio mention the fact that our two youngsters would like to have a dog. . . . It was a little cocker spaniel dog in a crate that he'd sent all the way from Texas, black and white, spotted. And our little girl Tricia, the six-year-old, named it 'Checkers.'"[4]
>
> —RICHARD NIXON, 1952

low blow, but the tactic resonated with Americans. The speech became known as the Checkers speech.

The Eisenhower Era

The Eisenhower-Nixon ticket won in November. As Eisenhower's vice president, Nixon played a similar role to the one he had in the campaign. He took a strong partisan stance and acted as a political lightning rod, allowing Eisenhower to preserve his image. However, the two men have been described as disliking each other, with Nixon thinking Eisenhower was too indecisive and Eisenhower thinking Nixon was too political.

Eisenhower's attitudes toward presidential power may have influenced his vice president. As president, Eisenhower made a decisive claim of executive privilege during the Army-McCarthy hearings of 1954, which concerned Senator Joseph McCarthy's accusations that officials of the US Army were engaged in acts of Communism and disloyalty to the United States. To protect the officials, Eisenhower wrote a letter to Defense Secretary Charles Wilson, instructing Wilson and his staff members to disregard subpoenas for the congressional hearings. John Adams, **counsel** for the US Army, presented Wilson's letter to Congress supporting Wilson's refusal to **testify** about a meeting between high-level White House officials. The letter detailed the historical precedents for executive privilege, and it was cited for years afterward as an authoritative defense of such a privilege.

Pursuit of the Presidency

Nixon easily won the Republican presidential nomination in 1960 but ended up losing in a very

counsel—A lawyer.
testify—To declare something in court under oath.

DIGNIFIED EXIT

John F. Kennedy won the 1960 election by fewer than 120,000 votes, the closest margin in popular votes since the 1884 presidential election.[5] Voting irregularities were alleged in Illinois and Texas, and some supporters urged Nixon to contest the results. However, Nixon conceded to Kennedy, explaining,

> I could think of no worse example for nations abroad, who for the first time were trying to put free electoral procedures into effect, than that of the United States wrangling over the results of our presidential election, and even suggesting that the presidency itself could be stolen by thievery at the ballot box.[6]

The gesture won him high praise at the time.

close election to Democrat John F. Kennedy, who was assassinated in 1963 and succeeded by Vice President Lyndon B. Johnson. After his defeat, Nixon took a job at a law firm and reemerged in politics in 1966 to campaign on behalf of Republican legislators. He once again started making headlines, attacking the policies of President Johnson, who had won the 1964 election. As the 1968 presidential election approached, the United States was in an era of upheaval. The country was being torn apart by disagreement over the Vietnam War (1954–1975). The civil rights movement was

mounting, culminating in the assassination of Martin Luther King Jr. in April 1968. Rioting, protests, and civil disobedience were sweeping the nation.

Amidst this chaos, Nixon seized on a theme of law and order for his presidential campaign. He supported increased police forces, a more powerful attorney general, increased use of wiretapping, and harsher penalties for criminals. He promised to end the Vietnam War, stop the draft, and curb illegal drug use. In contrast to his previous campaigns, Nixon stayed above the fray, letting running mate Spiro Agnew play the role of political attacker. Nixon narrowly defeated Democratic candidate Hubert Humphrey and third-party candidate George Wallace with 43.4 percent of the vote.[7] Voter turnout on Election Day, November 5, in 1968 was

JOHNSON'S WHITE HOUSE

Some historians believe the executive branch began to take on monarchical qualities beginning in the Eisenhower administration and continuing for several administrations. President Johnson, for example, was well known for micromanaging and controlling his staff. Former Johnson aide George Reedy described Johnson as being treated like a king: "No one speaks to him unless spoken to first. No one ever invites him to 'go soak your head' when his demands become too petulant and unreasonable."[8]

down from eight years prior, signifying the growing apathy and distrust Americans were feeling toward their government.

Nixon as President

While he had criticized Eisenhower for being too indecisive, some criticized President Nixon for being too controlling. House Republican leader Gerald Ford complained that the White House staff seemed to think Congress existed "only to follow their instructions, and we had no right to behave as a coequal branch of government."[9] Nixon's chief of staff, H. R. Haldeman,

KENNEDY AND JOHNSON

President Kennedy and his successor, Lyndon B. Johnson, both used executive privilege during their presidencies. When a Senate subcommittee asked for information regarding who edited the speeches of particular military personnel, Kennedy claimed executive privilege. However, he stated he would not claim the privilege indiscriminately and no privilege could be claimed by other White House staff members without his approval. "Each case must be judged on its own merits," Kennedy said.[10] Johnson continued this policy, telling a member of Congress, "The claim of 'executive privilege' will continue to be made only by the president."[11]

After losing the 1960 presidential election to Kennedy, Nixon campaigned again in 1968; this time, he won.

HANDS-ON PRESIDENT

Instead of delegating decision making, Nixon involved himself heavily in the particulars of running the White House and the country. He was concerned about every detail, from the White House curtains being open or closed, to seating arrangements at state dinners, to the photographs in his aides' offices. Because of this hands-on approach, many people later found it hard to believe Nixon had no knowledge of the cover-up that occurred concerning Watergate.

and another top aide, John Ehrlichman, acted as gatekeepers who restricted access to the president and carried out his wishes. The extent to which Nixon controlled his White House would not come out until the investigation into Watergate during his second term.

Nixon's domestic accomplishments included welfare reform, civil rights legislation, the first federal affirmative-action program, and economic stimulus. However, discontent continued growing over the Vietnam War. Nixon eventually reduced the number of American troops in Vietnam, but only after many more lives had been lost. The fighting in Southeast Asia expanded into Cambodia and Laos, setting off more protests in the United States. At one demonstration at Kent University in Ohio on May 4, 1970, National

Guard soldiers fired into the crowd. Four people were killed and nine wounded. Such incidents contributed to deepening disillusionment with the government. The US military did not fully exit Vietnam until 1973, and fighting continued in the country for several years after.

In 1971, as Nixon was struggling to extract the United States from the Vietnam War, a classified report known as the *Pentagon Papers* was released to the *New York Times* without authorization. The *Times* started publishing a series of articles on the report's information, which revealed the extent to which the previous four presidents had involved the United States in Southeast Asia since World War II. The US Department of Justice objected to the articles, claiming the information's continued release would harm national security interests, and the attorney general persuaded a federal court to issue a restraining order preventing further publication. The case made it to the Supreme Court, which decided 6–3 in favor of the newspaper, arguing Nixon had not provided enough proof that the information was too dangerous to release. The decision caused embarrassment for Nixon due to the content of the report and his inability to prevent its release, despite its top-secret classification.

Not everyone in Nixon's administration opposed the papers' release. Secretary of Defense Melvin Laird told Nixon 98 percent of the report could be released without creating problems, but Nixon disagreed, responding, "The era of negotiations can't succeed without secrecy."[12] The extent to which the president valued secrecy was about to become an even greater issue. ∼

Chapter 4

Watergate Erupts

*A*s his first term as president was coming to a close, Nixon was worried about his reelection chances. To give himself an edge in his campaign, Nixon made several attempts to sabotage his potential Democratic challengers. When Democratic nominee George Wallace was running for governor of Alabama that year, Nixon contributed $400,000 to Wallace's challenger in the Democratic primary. Wallace won the governorship anyway, setting him up well to run for president. However, after an attempt was made on Wallace's life, he dropped out of the presidential race. Because of the assassination attempt on Wallace, the Secret Service assigned a security detail to another potential nominee, Senator Ed Kennedy. Nixon had members of the detail report back to

him on Kennedy's activities. A White House security staffer hired a private investigator to compile evidence that might be damaging, such as Kennedy cheating on his wife or engaging in other illicit activities. When Kennedy appeared to be a serious candidate, Nixon had Secret Service agents tail the senator.

Questionable Activities

Meanwhile, Nixon supported the rise of eventual Democratic presidential nominee George McGovern, who Republicans felt would be the weakest candidate and therefore the easiest to beat in an election. During the course of the election, the Committee to Reelect the President (CRP) engaged in a number of questionable activities, which included forging documents and leaking false information. These activities did not come to light until the investigation of the Watergate scandal. Former attorney general John Mitchell led the CRP, and a number of White House staffers participated directly or indirectly in the organization, including counsel to the president Charles Colson and White House aides Dwight Chapin and Jeb Magruder.

The CRP's most notorious operation was breaking into the Democratic National Headquarters at the

Carl Bernstein, *left*, and Bob Woodward, *right*, reported on the Watergate scandal for the *Washington Post*.

Watergate complex on June 17, 1972. A night watchman alerted police, who arrested the five men attempting to plant surveillance equipment in the offices. Three of the men formerly worked for the Central Intelligence Agency (CIA), while a fourth was currently on the CIA payroll, and a fifth—James McCord—was a former CIA agent who worked as chief of security for the CRP. Two other men, E. Howard Hunt and G. Gordon Liddy,

WOODWARD AND BERNSTEIN

As soon as the Watergate break-ins occurred, *Washington Post* reporters Bob Woodward and Carl Bernstein started reporting on the incident's connection to the White House. Their stories were based on information from an anonymous source known as Deep Throat, who in 2005 was identified as Federal Bureau of Investigation (FBI) official Mark Felt. Their Pulitzer Prize–winning reporting from the summer of 1972 through Nixon's resignation in 1974 linked the Watergate burglaries to high-level officials in the Nixon administration and helped focus the public's attention on the wrongdoing in the White House. Their investigation was an example of the media playing a watchdog role. While not mentioned as such in the Constitution, investigative reporting provides another check on the branches of government.

were taken into custody at a hotel across the street, where they had been coordinating the break-in with the others. Hunt and Liddy were former White House aides who had gone on to work for the CRP. Within days, *Washington Post* reporters Carl Bernstein and Bob Woodward began publishing articles about connections between the break-in and the Nixon White House. The publicity prompted Nixon to call a press conference, in which he stated, "the White House has had no involvement in this particular incident."[1]

The scandal took many months to pick up steam. Hunt, Liddy, and the five burglars were indicted in the grand jury hearings on September 15, but the trial was not scheduled until after the presidential election. Judge John Sirica issued a gag order, meaning participants in the case were not allowed to discuss it with the media.

In the meantime, Wallace dropped out of the race, and McGovern became the Democratic nominee. McGovern was so unpopular that his approval numbers started falling immediately after the Democratic convention, a time when most candidates receive an increase in popularity. Coming out of the Republican convention, Nixon held a lead of 39 percent over McGovern, but he continued fund-raising and

CONGRESSIONAL ELECTION

Democrats did well in the 1972 congressional elections; Republicans gained only 12 seats in the House and lost two seats in the Senate. The Democrats' majority in both houses of Congress became important when Nixon came under investigation during the Watergate scandal. The Democrats focused their investigation on the Republican president and did not expand it to encompass questionable activities of candidates from both parties, as Republicans at the time were urging.

campaigning in an effort to achieve a decisive victory on Election Day.[2] His efforts paid off; Nixon defeated McGovern in a landslide victory on November 7, 1972.

The Burglary Trial

The men implicated in the White House burglary were tried from January 8 to January 30, 1973, on charges of burglary, conspiracy, and interception of wire and oral communications. A jury found Liddy and McCord guilty on all counts, while Hunt and the other four burglars pleaded guilty before going to trial. Judge Sirica expressed his skepticism that a complete picture of what happened had been presented at trial and expressed support for an inquiry to be conducted by the Senate. He stated, "I am still not satisfied that all the pertinent facts that might be available—I say might be available— have been produced before an American jury."[3]

On February 7, the Senate voted to conduct its own investigation into Watergate. Senator Samuel Ervin led the push to create the seven-member Select Committee on Presidential Campaign Activities, which he was then chosen to lead. As the committee, which became known as the Ervin committee, began investigating, another detail came to light. L. Patrick Gray, a candidate to lead

the Federal Bureau of Investigation (FBI), inadvertently revealed that he had met with John Dean, counsel to the president, and given the White House access to the FBI's investigation reports on Watergate. In response to the revelation of this meeting, which tied the president to Watergate, Nixon invoked executive privilege for the first time concerning Watergate. He instructed Dean and other members of his staff not to testify at the Senate committee hearings.

While Nixon had managed to keep the Watergate scandal under control during his campaign the previous fall, it was exploding by the spring of 1973. On March 19, just days before the Watergate burglars' sentencing, defendant McCord had a letter delivered to Judge Sirica. Sirica read the letter to the court at the

SAMUEL ERVIN

Samuel Ervin was a Democratic senator from North Carolina from 1954 to 1974. A graduate of Harvard Law School, he was known for conservative leanings and for being a strict constructionist, meaning he supported a narrow interpretation of the Constitution. Before leading the congressional Watergate investigation, he was best known for serving on the committee that investigated Senator Joseph McCarthy.

The Watergate complex in Washington DC was the site of the burglary Nixon was accused of covering up.

sentencing hearing on March 23. In it, McCord alleged, "political pressure was applied to the defendants to plead guilty and remain silent."[4] He went on to assert that witnesses in the trial had **perjured** themselves and that "others in the Watergate operation were not identified."[5] A week later, McCord identified presidential staff members Dean, Mitchell, Colson, Magruder, and Haldeman as having had knowledge of or involvement in the Watergate burglary and cover-up. Fearful he would be made the administration's scapegoat, Dean agreed to talk to **prosecutors**. Magruder admitted to perjuring himself during the previous September's grand jury hearing regarding the burglaries. Other participants also began trying to negotiate deals with prosecutors.

Call for a Special Prosecutor

Facing increasing pressure from the press, the public, and Congress, Nixon allowed White House aides to testify before the Ervin committee. He accepted resignations from Dean, Haldeman, and other officials implicated in the new testimony, including one of Nixon's top

perjured—Violated an oath by knowingly giving false testimony.
prosecutor—A lawyer who brings legal action against someone.

aides, John Ehrlichman, and US Attorney General
Richard Kleindienst.

Denying any knowledge of wrongdoing, Nixon
promised to cooperate with an investigation into his
administration's involvement in the Watergate incident.
On May 1, Congress
passed legislation
providing for the
appointment of a
special prosecutor.
Kleindienst had
resigned on
April 30, and
congressional leaders
informed Nixon his
choice for the new
attorney general,
Elliot Richardson,
would be confirmed
only if a suitable special prosecutor were identified.

> "When one speaks about public confidence and trust, that is the heart of the matter: people are entitled to something more than confidence that their highest public officials do not break the law; they are also entitled to know that these officials do not lie and cheat and corrupt the institutions of government."[6]
>
> —*A* WASHINGTON POST *EDITORIAL, WRITTEN IN REACTION TO NIXON'S PROMISE TO LAUNCH AN INVESTIGATION INTO WATERGATE*

Taped conversations later revealed Nixon intended
the investigation to be for appearance's sake only and
not to actually uncover the truth about Watergate.
"This is not to prosecute the case," the president assured

Haldeman before his resignation. "A special prosecutor to look at the indictments, to see that the indictments run to everybody they need to run to. So that it isn't to the president's men, you see."[7] Richardson was questioned intently about his intentions toward the Watergate investigation during his confirmation hearing. Richardson promised the **Senate Judiciary Committee** the prosecutor would act independently, and he would not fire the prosecutor unless his actions were "arbitrary, capricious, and unreasonable."[8] He knew his nomination was in danger of not being confirmed if he did not find a suitable special prosecutor.

After several of his first choices declined, Richardson turned to Archibald Cox, a well-respected legal mind who had served in the Kennedy administration. Richardson and Cox agreed on a set of guidelines for the position, including that Richardson could dismiss Cox for "extraordinary improprieties" only.[9] Cox also asked for the power to investigate any presidential appointee or White House staff member, to which Richardson agreed. Reassured that Cox could

Senate Judiciary Committee—A standing Senate committee that conducts hearings prior to major Senate votes, including amendments and federal judge appointments.

ARCHIBALD COX

Archibald Cox was not Attorney General Elliot Richardson's first choice to serve as special prosecutor in the Watergate case. Richardson had wanted to appoint someone with more extensive criminal trial experience, but four other prospects turned down the position before he asked Cox. Richardson finally approached Cox because of his reputation as an independent thinker who was widely respected in the legal field.

Cox had a long career in academia and government leading up to his appointment as special prosecutor for the Watergate case. He headed the Wage Stabilization Board under President Harry Truman. When John F. Kennedy was a senator, Cox was a key adviser who helped him write legislation and went on to compose speeches for him during his presidential campaign. During Kennedy's presidency, Cox served as solicitor general, the attorney who represents the US federal government in the US Supreme Court.

investigate without interference, on May 25 the Senate Judiciary Committee approved Richardson's nomination for attorney general on the condition he make good on his promise to appoint Cox as special prosecutor.

However, Cox's idea of what his role as special prosecutor would be was different from Nixon's. Standing before the Senate Judiciary Committee in the spring of 1973, Cox promised that as special prosecutor,

Archibald Cox was sworn in as special prosecutor in May 1973.

he would do whatever it took to get to the bottom of
the Watergate scandal, regardless of how high up the
corruption and cover-up went. Senator Robert Byrd
questioned: "Even though that trail should lead, Heaven

forbid, to the Oval Office of the White House itself?" Cox answered him with conviction: "Wherever that trail may lead."[10] ~

Chapter 5

The Investigation

The president and his administration were facing investigation from all sides: Congress, the media, and now the special prosecutor. After the Ervin committee started hearing testimony on May 17, 1973, Nixon tried to control the damage by issuing a lengthy statement on May 22, in which he stated, "I took no part in, nor was I aware of, any subsequent efforts that may have been made to cover up Watergate."[1]

Newly appointed Special Prosecutor Cox assembled a staff and threw himself into the investigation, building on evidence already assembled by the Ervin committee. The accumulating evidence suggested the administration's wrongdoing far surpassed the Watergate burglary. The evidence also

The Senate committee began hearings regarding the Watergate scandal in the spring of 1973.

pointed to White House involvement in the 1971 break-in of a psychiatrist's office. The burglars were in search of medical records that would discredit Daniel Ellsberg, the military analyst who had leaked the *Pentagon Papers*. Cox's team also investigated a group of Nixon's staff members, known as the Plumbers, who were charged with identifying and taking care of information leaks in the administration. Other information pointed to the administration's illegal interference in other government agencies and campaign finance law violations. However, the connections were difficult to prove. Through interviews with a White House aide, Cox became aware of tapes containing recordings of the president's meetings and conversations that could help Cox build his case.

PRESIDENTIAL RECORDINGS

Several other presidents made a habit of recording their conversations. Franklin Roosevelt taped some conversations for the purpose of keeping an accurate historical record. Truman made a few recordings before deciding to discontinue the practice. Eisenhower admitted to taping conversations so he later would be able to prove definitively what he did or did not say. Kennedy made a habit of secretly taping meetings. Johnson had recording systems in the Oval Office and Cabinet Room of which his aides were aware.

Starting on June 25, former White House counsel John Dean began five days of testimony before the Ervin committee. He described meetings he had with Nixon following the Watergate break-in to plan the cover-up. The plans included making payments to the burglars to keep their silence regarding the others involved in the break-in. Dean supported his testimony with documents and provided dates for when he had met with the president. Republican Senator Howard Baker asked him a question that has since become famous: "What did the president know, and when did he know it?"[2] However, Haldeman, Ehrlichman, and Mitchell all testified in support of President Nixon's account of the break-in, in which he denied all knowledge. When the committee requested records that might have confirmed or denied details of the testimony, the president claimed executive privilege, writing on July 7: "No president could function if the private papers of his office, prepared by his personal staff, were open to public scrutiny."[3]

Standoff over the Tapes

The following week, testimony confirmed the existence of the tapes Cox had learned of from the aide. Investigators believed these would show definitively what the president had known and when he knew it. Cox's

team determined which tapes would be most relevant by examining logs of presidential meetings and determining which meetings most likely related to Watergate. One of the requested tapes contained a June 20, 1972, meeting between Nixon, Haldeman, and Ehrlichman. It was the first White House meeting between the president and his top aides since the break-in, so it was likely they had discussed Watergate. Cox's team also focused on tapes containing meetings featuring content that had already been publicly discussed by the president and his staff. This would undermine Nixon's assertions of confidentiality.

In early July, the Ervin committee requested the president turn over the tapes. Cox made the same request on July 18, 1973. Nixon denied both requests, citing executive privilege. In the case of the Senate committee, Nixon was citing the separation of powers contained in the US Constitution as a basis for executive privilege, that one

> "If you are an ordinary prosecutor, and thus a part of the Executive branch as well as an officer of the court, you are subject to the instructions of your superior, up to and including the President, and can have access to Presidential papers only as and if the President sees fit to make them available to you."[4]
>
> —CHARLES ALAN WRIGHT, LAWYER FOR NIXON

branch should not be able to interfere with another. Cox had argued separation of powers did not pertain to the special prosecutor's request because he was in the same branch of government as the president. Charles Alan Wright, lawyer for the president, countered this by pointing out that Cox was the president's subordinate.

Quest for a Subpoena

Cox considered his options. He knew if he subpoenaed the materials from the president, the case would likely be challenged and taken to the US Supreme Court. He questioned whether the Supreme Court, with four justices who had been appointed by Nixon, would vote to take the case. If it did take the case, the court might rule to uphold executive privilege, in which case Nixon would not be forced to hand over the tapes. If the court sided with Nixon, Cox would lose all hope of acquiring the evidence he needed. If the Supreme Court upheld the subpoena, Cox was unsure Nixon would abide by such a ruling, and he did not know how the court might enforce its will if Nixon simply refused. The country had never experienced a situation in which a sitting president might be arrested. This was also the furthest degree to which executive privilege had been challenged.

Having committed to following through with his investigation regardless of where it led, Cox subpoenaed the tapes on July 23. He decided to subpoena the nine tapes most likely to contain information directly relevant to his case. They would serve as a test. If the subpoena was upheld, additional tapes could be requested later. Ervin issued his own subpoena, the first time Congress had subpoenaed a president since 1807. Within days, the president responded he would not be honoring either subpoena. The two sides would go to court over the issue. Ervin would use the refusal to comply with his subpoena as grounds to impeach Nixon. Cox's team assembled all of their arguments and evidence in support of the subpoena into a brief.

In the meantime, a new grand jury convened in August 1973 to hear evidence concerning the different investigations related to Watergate, including the break-in at the psychiatrist's office, perjury, the campaign contributions cases, and other alleged crimes. The grand jury was preparing to make decisions on whom to indict for these crimes. The officials set to be indicted included White House counsel John Dean and members of the Plumbers, including Egil Krogh, John Ehrlichman, and Charles Colson.

On August 22, Cox and Wright appeared before district court judge Sirica to present their arguments on why the tapes should or should not be released. Both lawyers cited precedents to support their sides. Wright pointed out that no previous president had been asked to fulfill such a significant request for a release of private information.

Cox cited Wright's own writings on the subject, which argued that the courts can decide when to apply executive privilege. One of the precedents he cited was

ISSUING THE SUBPOENA

When subpoenaing the president's tapes, the special prosecutor's office was careful to serve the subpoena correctly, knowing a technicality could derail the entire case later on if the president claimed he had not received the subpoena. Philip Lacovara, a lawyer working for the special prosecutor's office, and legal assistant Peter Kreindler delivered the subpoena personally. They delivered it to Special White House Counsel Fred Buzhardt. Lacovara conversed with Buzhardt for ten minutes so he could later say for certain he had delivered the subpoena to the right person. On the back of the document, Buzhardt wrote, "Received by J. Fred Buzhardt, special counsel to the president."[5] Lacovara asked him to add the words "on behalf of the president," so there could be no question the subpoena had been served to the president.[6]

JUDGE JOHN SIRICA

President Dwight Eisenhower appointed John Sirica, a Republican, as a district court judge for the District of Columbia in 1957. In 1971, Sirica became the court's chief judge. A former boxer, Sirica's reputation for toughness as a judge earned him the nickname "Maximum John." He has been both praised and criticized for his handling of the Watergate trials. In a 1992 obituary of Sirica, a *Washington Post* reporter wrote:

> *Throughout his conduct of the Watergate trials, Sirica made it clear he intended to get at the truth of what had happened, and said that in doing so, he did not intend to be bound by traditional ideas of courtroom procedures. He often questioned witnesses himself, and he instructed jurors that it was their duty to consider not just what had happened, but why. When he suspected that what was unfolding in his courtroom was less than the whole truth, he made his feelings known.[8]*

US v. Clark, in which the court ruled that secret jury deliberations could be scrutinized if wrongdoing was suspected. "We think this case is precisely similar," Cox argued. "There is not merely accusation, but stronger reason to believe that the integrity of the executive office has been corrupted, although the extent of the rot is not yet clear."[7]

Judge Sirica supported Cox and ordered Nixon to turn over the tapes.

Judge Sirica ruled a week later, on August 29, that the president must turn over the nine tapes being requested by Cox to the court so the judge could determine whether their content should be privileged. Instead of supplying the tapes, Nixon appealed the decision. Wright and Cox repeated their arguments before a panel of judges at the US Court of Appeals for the District of Columbia. Two of the conservative judges recused themselves, leaving five judges to hear the case. Under questioning by the judges, Wright argued such tapes should not be subpoenaed under any circumstances, even if the president was suspected of a crime. Wright stated:

> It seems to me that so long as the President says 'I participated in these in the exercise of my constitutional duty and not as part of a cover-up, not as part of a criminal scheme,' that is not for the courts, the grand jury, the special prosecutor to say, 'Mr. President, we don't believe you. We think you are a criminal.' I think that if there is reason to suspect the President of criminal conduct, that it is necessary to go to the one remedy that the Constitution has provided for that purpose.[9]

IMPEACHMENT

Impeachment refers to the congressional proceedings that remove an elected official from office. After the House of Representatives passes a resolution to conduct an inquiry, the House Judiciary Committee investigates whether sufficient grounds exist to warrant articles of impeachment, the charges brought against the elected official. Then the full House debates the articles of impeachment and votes on each article. Once the House passes the final list of articles, the official has been impeached, meaning the official is subject to a trial in the Senate. The chief justice of the Supreme Court presides over the trial, while the Senate acts as jury. A two-thirds majority of the Senate is needed to remove the official from office.

The constitutional remedy Wright referred to was impeachment, in which Congress would hold special proceedings to consider removing Nixon from office. Cox repeated his arguments, as well, after which one of the judges questioned whether a sitting president could be arrested for **contempt**, and if not, whether the court's decision had any relevance. Cox had also worried about this issue but responded that the court should decide

contempt—Willful disobedience or disrespect of a judge, court, or legislative body.

the case on its merits, not on its ability to enforce the outcome.

The judges knew if they sided with the president, they could be setting the precedent that all presidential records could be kept secret or that the courts did not have the power to rule on such issues. Instead, the court issued a memorandum urging the two sides, as mutual members of the executive branch, to reach a solution on their own. The court asked them to reach a compromise by September 20.

> "Our country is blessed of course . . . by the fact that Presidents, when the time came, have always bowed to a decision of the Supreme Court and complied with it."[10]
>
> —*ARCHIBALD COX*

Nixon's lawyers offered to provide summaries of the tapes written in the third person. Cox made a counterproposal involving partial transcripts and an objective third party that could verify the parts of the tape not transcribed were not relevant. Nixon's team did not accept the counterproposal, and the two sides failed to reach a compromise by September 20.

Hearing this, the US court of appeals judges took several weeks before handing down a decision. When they finally did on October 12, they ruled in favor of the special prosecutor. The opinion stated that while presidential communications are usually privileged, the judges did not agree with the president's lawyer's claim that this privilege was absolute. In this case, the court found the special prosecutor had demonstrated compelling reasons for overriding the privilege. The opinion also noted that Nixon had already yielded his privilege of communications privacy in letting his aides testify before Congress during the 1973 hearings of the Ervin committee. In cases where details related to national security might be revealed, the court instructed Judge Sirica to inspect the tapes as needed. The court had definitively ruled against the president, but Nixon was not ready to yield to its decision. ∼

Chapter 6

Subpoenas and Showdowns

*D*espite Sirica's order to release the tapes, Nixon's and Cox's teams continued to wrangle over the release of the tapes through October 1973. During the same month, the United States faced a conflict in the Middle East when Egypt and Syria, backed by the Soviet Union, attacked Israel, a US ally. Nixon's advisers believed the Soviets were taking advantage of Nixon's distraction over Watergate. Nixon believed Soviet President Leonid Brezhnev would view it as a sign of weakness if Nixon could not control Cox. To further add to the cloud surrounding Nixon's presidency, Vice President Agnew resigned from office on October 10 following charges of

bribes, tax evasion, and other criminal activities. Nixon appointed Gerald Ford, House Republican leader, to replace Agnew as vice president.

Nixon's Compromise

As the court's deadline to turn over the tapes grew nearer, Nixon proposed a compromise in which he would provide summaries of the nine tapes. Senator John Stennis would listen to the tapes to verify their content matched the summaries. However, Stennis was known to be hard of hearing. The president's proposal also was contingent on the fact that the prosecutor's office could not request any additional materials.

Cox held a press conference, explaining why he could not accept Nixon's compromise. Cox pointed out that depending on any one man to interpret evidence on a matter so important was highly inappropriate, and it would be ineffective to try any case on anything but the best evidence. He also detailed the months of difficulties he had experienced trying to gain cooperation from the Nixon administration.

On October 20, Cox held a press conference rejecting Nixon's compromise; hours later, Cox was fired in the Saturday Night Massacre.

The Saturday Night Massacre

Angered by the response, Nixon ordered Attorney General Richardson to fire his special prosecutor later that day, Saturday, October 20, 1973. Because Richardson had made an agreement with the Senate Judiciary Committee to dismiss the prosecutor for extreme improprieties only, Richardson resigned instead of carrying out the order. Nixon then ordered Deputy

THE PRESS CONFERENCE

The journalists at the press conference in which Cox rejected the president's proposed compromise were described by some as being unusually supportive. Instead of hammering him with questions, the normally hard-hitting Washington press corps seemed practically in awe of the stand Cox was taking against the president. Near the end of the conference, journalist Sarah McClendon stood up to ask:

> Sir, you are rather unique in history because you personally rebuffed the president of the United States. And you come here today hand-holding with your wife, and it took a lot of moral courage. . . . My question is, how could you expect to succeed in this job? How could you expect to succeed?[1]

"I thought it was worth a try," answered Cox. "I thought it was important. If it could be done, I thought it would help the country; and if I lost, what the hell.[2]

Attorney General William Ruckelshaus to fire Cox, and Ruckelshaus reacted by resigning as well. Solicitor General Robert Bork became acting head of the Justice Department. Bork, too, wanted to resign, but his predecessors convinced him to stay so the entire Justice Department was not in disarray. Bork carried out the president's wishes and dismissed Cox from his job as special prosecutor.

The protesters gathered outside the White House following the Saturday Night Massacre were a clear indication of the poor public opinion of Nixon.

The events of the weekend became known in the media as the Saturday Night Massacre. The resignations and firings quickly ignited a firestorm of criticism of President Nixon. Many people did not think the president was above the law and were angered by Nixon's refusal to cooperate with legal proceedings. By Sunday morning, protesters began gathering outside the White House wearing Nixon masks and prison stripes. The next

day, Congress received approximately 150,000 telegrams. Within ten days, that number had tripled. Almost unanimously, the people who wrote in opposed Cox's firing. Many called for Nixon's impeachment. As outrage over the incident swept the country, the president's approval rating fell to 17 percent.[3]

New Prosecutor

Nixon may have hoped firing the investigator would end the investigation, but that was not the case. Instead, the Saturday Night Massacre only intensified the focus on the president because it appeared he was hiding something serious. In response to the mounting pressure, the president publicly stated he would turn over the requested tapes. He also moved to appoint a new special prosecutor, knowing if he did not, Congress might appoint a special prosecutor of its choosing.

Nixon's staff contacted Leon Jaworski, a political conservative who was well known in Washington. Jaworski had been one of the lawyers who turned down Attorney General Richardson before Cox was hired. Like Cox, Jaworski had concerns that the special prosecutor would not be able to operate with enough independence. The Saturday Night Massacre had only heightened

Nixon's popularity plummeted following the Saturday Night Massacre, and the accumulating evidence against him kept him on the defense.

those concerns. Alexander Haig, Nixon's new chief of staff, assured Jaworski he would operate with even more independence than Cox. Unlike Cox, the new special prosecutor could be fired only with the approval of a panel of eight congressional leaders and members of the Senate and House Judiciary Committees. In his memoir, Jaworski wrote that with this requirement in place, he felt he would be able to operate with sufficient

independence. He also knew Congress's appointing of a prosecutor instead of Nixon would likely take months of search and debate, delaying a resolution to the Watergate matter. Jaworski also questioned whether Congress had the constitutional power to appoint someone who would serve in the executive branch. With these factors in mind, Jaworski decided to accept the position of special prosecutor.

By now, the investigative team formerly led by Cox had already obtained guilty pleas from several parties, including White House counsel John Dean and several high-level CRP operatives, including Jeb Magruder. The task force had collected evidence that could lead to more indictments, convictions, or guilty pleas—but only if supporting evidence could be obtained. Like his predecessor, Jaworski knew he needed to get the relevant tapes to cement his case.

By late October, Judge Sirica had still not received the nine tapes he had ordered Nixon to release. The matter came to a head after the grand jury indictment of Egil Krogh, who had led the White House task force known as the Plumbers. Krogh was indicted on charges related to perjury and to the break-in at Daniel Ellsberg's psychiatrist's offices. Krogh's lawyers were

JAWORSKI'S POSITION

When discussing whether to take the job of special prosecutor with White House Chief of Staff Alexander Haig, Jaworski warned Haig that he had already taken a public stance on the Watergate matter. Several weeks before Cox had been appointed as special prosecutor, Jaworski gave a speech at a meeting of lawyers in Texas in which he praised the actions of Judge Sirica and supported a full and thorough investigation. "I've taken a public position since this affair started that it should be thoroughly investigated and publicized," Jaworski told Haig. "And I feel that every person criminally involved should be prosecuted. If I take this job, I'm going to work that way." Haig responded, "That's just what we want."[4]

moving to dismiss the charges on the grounds that his actions had been based on an interest in national security. The special prosecutor's task force submitted a brief to the hearing that Jaworski felt got at the heart of the conflict between his office and the president's. The brief emphasized that national security was not a valid justification for criminal acts and that the president was not above the law. The brief stated:

> The debate over what may be done in the name
> of "national security" has taken a more ambitious
> turn. It has been advanced by low-level personnel
> to justify an illegal break-in for the installation

of microphones in the offices of the Democratic National Committee. . . . While the claim of national security gives these claims of legalized burglary a deceptively compelling ring, ultimately they rest on a wholesale rejection of the rule of law

EGIL KROGH

Egil Krogh, leader of the Plumbers, eventually agreed to cooperate with the special prosecutor's task force. According to Jaworski, the young lawyer decided national security did not excuse his involvement in breaking into the office of Ellsberg's psychiatrist. Hoping for leniency, Krogh provided Jaworski with details of the break-in. Krogh and another Plumber had drafted a memo recommending a covert operation to obtain the psychiatrist's files, and Ehrlichman approved the plan. Krogh also gave $5,000 to White House and campaign aid G. Gordon Liddy, who arranged the break-in. When pleading guilty, Krogh told the court:

> *My coming to this point today stems from my asking myself what ideas I wanted to stand for, what I wanted to represent to myself and to my family and to be identified with for the rest of my experience. I simply feel that what was done in the Ellsberg operation was in violation of what I perceive to be a fundamental idea in the character of this country—the paramount importance of the rights of the individual. I don't want to be associated with that violation any longer by attempting to defend it.*[5]

INTERFERENCE FROM CONGRESS

Some people still questioned whether Special Prosecutor Jaworski could operate with enough independence, even with the new guidelines. While Jaworski continued his investigation, both the Senate and the House of Representatives were considering legislation that would enable Congress to appoint its own independent prosecutor for Watergate. A *Washington Post* editorial argued that by debating the issue, Congress was potentially undermining Jaworski's effectiveness. Soon after the editorial ran, both the Senate and the House dropped the bills.

and espouse a doctrine that government officials may ignore the requirements of positive criminal statutes when they feel the circumstances dictate.[6]

While Krogh's motion hearing was taking place, Jaworski reiterated his request for the tapes to Nixon's lawyers. The political pressure on Nixon was mounting, and he agreed to turn over some of the tapes. However, two of the nine subpoenaed tapes were reported missing, and the recording from June 20, 1972, contained an 18-and-a-half-minute gap. This tape was considered especially important because it captured the first meeting between Ehrlichman, Haldeman, and the president following the Watergate break-in. Haldeman's notes on the meeting indicated the men had discussed Watergate.

However, there was no mention of Watergate in the recording, suggesting that particular conversation may have been in the missing portion. Fred Buzhardt, one of the president's lawyers, informed Jaworski of the situation, and the two arranged to meet with Judge Sirica in his chambers. Sirica decided to call another hearing in which experts would be called upon to examine the tapes. These experts asserted the gap had not been caused accidentally.

Need for Evidence

In December 1973, five months after Cox first subpoenaed the tapes, the special prosecutor's team, now led by Jaworski, finally heard the first segments of the recordings. Nixon's staff had submitted the tapes to Judge Sirica, who then released selected segments pertaining to the investigation to the special prosecutor's office. The first segment Jaworski listened to contained Nixon, Haldeman, and Dean discussing monetary payments to be made to the Watergate burglars in exchange for the cooperation in a cover-up. The president also could be heard instructing his chief of staff on how to avoid perjuring himself. For the first time, Jaworski realized how directly involved the president was in the crimes and the cover-up. But he

needed access to more of the tapes to be fully prepared to bring indictments against top-level officials and even, potentially, Nixon himself.

Much of the administration's wrongdoing had come to light during the Ervin hearings in the winter of 1973. Additionally, in February, the House Judiciary Committee had begun its own investigation into the president's possible impeachment. But the special prosecutor needed additional evidence that would stand up in a court of law. "It was a Special Prosecution Force rule that we not seek an indictment unless we believed there was a 50 percent chance of obtaining a conviction," Jaworski wrote in his memoir. "We decided we didn't have that standard of evidence."[7] To achieve such a standard, Jaworski identified additional tapes he thought would be needed for the prosecution, but the White House continued failing to provide them. Jaworski threatened additional court action if the administration did not turn over the tapes. In response, the president's lawyers turned over some of the tapes, but not all.

Evidence was mounting in support of Nixon's involvement in various crimes, including obstruction of justice, conspiracy, wiretapping, perjury, burglary, election fraud, money laundering, and bribery. Jaworski

had to decide whether to pursue an indictment of the president. The grand jury was charged with handing down indictments, but to be valid, the special prosecutor had to sign each indictment. Jaworski explained in his memoir,

> *I did not believe the US Supreme Court would permit indictment of a sitting President for obstruction of justice—especially when the House Judiciary Committee was then engaged in an inquiry into whether the President should be impeached on that very ground. . . . The proper constitutional process, it seemed to me, would be for the Committee to proceed first with its impeachment inquiry.*[8]

Subjecting the president to both a criminal trial and an impeachment proceeding at the same time could violate Nixon's right to a fair trial, Jaworski reasoned. He also worried that putting the president on trial would subject the country to many more months of the Watergate scandal. Jaworski decided to name the president as an **unindicted coconspirator**. This would eventually

---

unindicted coconspirator—Someone who is named in an indictment as having participated in a conspiracy but who is not charged with any crime.

permit the tape recordings made by the president to be entered into evidence. However, Jaworski decided to delay an announcement of this until closer to the trial, after the House had conducted impeachment proceedings, because the information might influence the impeachment trial.

In January 1974, Haig conveyed to the special prosecutor's task force that the president had released all of the evidence that would be forthcoming. The president reiterated this stance in his State of the Union address. Nixon also got a new attorney; he replaced Charles Wright with James St. Clair, who had decades of trial experience in high-profile cases.

In March, Haldeman, Ehrlichman, Mitchell, and four other officials were indicted for their participation in the Watergate cover-up. Ehrlichman and others were indicted for charges related to the psychiatrist's office burglary. Needing further evidence to go to trial, in April, Jaworski subpoenaed 64 more tapes, while the House Judiciary Committee subpoenaed 42 tapes. Judge Sirica upheld the subpoena and ordered Nixon to turn over the tapes. The president responded to this request by submitting more than 1,000 pages of heavily edited transcripts on April 30. "Never before in [the] history of the Presidency have records that are so private been

Nixon gestures toward the transcripts he turned over to the prosecution instead of the subpoenaed tapes.

made public," Nixon told Americans. "In giving you these records—blemishes and all—I am placing my trust in the fairness of the American people."[9]

When Sirica maintained that Nixon still needed to honor the subpoena for the tapes, St. Clair challenged the decision in the US court of appeals. To avoid further delays to the trial, and since the court of appeals had already ruled on a similar subpoena during Cox's tenure, Jaworski appealed directly to the Supreme Court on May 24. On May 31, the Supreme Court announced it had accepted the case. ～

Chapter 7

The Supreme Court

As the Supreme Court hearing approached, the tide of public opinion was quickly turning against the president. In June 1974, *Washington Post* reporters Woodward and Bernstein published their account of the Watergate burglaries and associated crimes in a book called *All the President's Men.* Support from both Republicans and Democrats was growing for Nixon's impeachment. However, the Supreme Court was only taking up one issue: whether the president had to turn over the 64 tapes Jaworski had subpoenacd as evidence. Jaworski believed that without the tapes, the country would never know the extent of the Watergate crimes and cover-up

DUE PROCESS

The US Constitution guarantees no person can be "deprived of life, liberty or property without due process of law."[1] The Fifth Amendment establishes due process for the federal government, while the Fourteenth Amendment applies it to state governments. Due process means all citizens are required to receive fair treatment within the legal system. When Jaworski named Nixon as an unindicted coconspirator in Watergate, Jaworski was publicly accusing Nixon of a crime, even though the president would not be formally charged with the crime. Because of this accusation, St. Clair believed Congress would be biased against Nixon, which could result in an unfair trial and deprive the president of his right to due process of the law.

operation. Both Jaworski's and Nixon's teams recognized that the court's decision was likely to directly affect the Watergate hearings and the impeachment trial.

Each side had until June 21 to submit its brief to the court in advance of the July 8 hearing date. Their arguments concerned three main questions: whether the court had the legal power to decide a conflict within the executive branch, whether the president had an executive privilege allowing him to protect communications within his branch, and, if so, whether the public

interest in obtaining that evidence warranted overriding that privilege.

St. Clair's Legal Brief

St. Clair's brief focused on whether or not it was appropriate for the court to intervene in the dispute. He argued that strictly enforcing the boundaries separating the branches of government was important to the long-term well-being of the nation:

> *All other considerations are secondary because preserving the integrity of the separation of powers is vital to the preservation of our Constitution as a living body of fundamental law. If the arguments*

JAMES ST. CLAIR

As the Watergate investigation intensified, President Nixon realized he needed a lawyer with more experience trying criminal cases. In January 1974, he replaced Charles Wright with James St. Clair, who had decades of trial experience in high-profile cases. St. Clair had represented a Yale University chaplain accused of helping students avoid the draft, and he represented Boston Public Schools in a lawsuit regarding desegregation of schools. In response to the criticism he received for representing the president, St. Clair explained, "I don't represent Mr. Nixon personally. I represent him in his capacity as president."[2]

James St. Clair, *center*, defended Nixon in the Supreme Court hearing of *The United States v. Nixon*.

of the Special Prosecutor were to prevail, the constitutional balance would be altered in ways that no one alive today could predict or measure.[3]

Although the subpoenas being challenged in court were the special prosecutor's, not the House Judiciary Committee's, St. Clair argued that the dual investigations were linked so the Supreme Court's decision would affect the impeachment proceedings. Because impeachment is a constitutional power of Congress, part of the **legislative branch**, St. Clair asserted that it would be inappropriate for the Supreme Court, part of the judicial branch, to intervene. According to his brief,

> *The processes—each with an entirely different history, function, and structure—have become intertwined, and the resulting confusion, both conceptual and procedural, is manifestly unfair to the President as an individual and harmful to the relationship between his office and the legislative branch.*[4]

Despite Jaworski's intention to hold off on the naming of the president as an unindicted coconspirator

legislative branch—One of three branches of the federal government; it includes the US Congress and makes laws.

until closer to the trial, his plan had been leaked to the press. St. Clair argued the naming of the president as an unindicted coconspirator was prejudicial in the House Judiciary Committee's proceedings, and consequently, the president was being denied due process.

St. Clair also argued that because the special prosecutor and president work in the executive branch of government, court intervention in a dispute between them would violate the separation of powers. Furthermore, St. Clair's brief maintained that the special prosecutor had not established a "unique and compelling need" to override the president's executive privilege.[5] Finally, the brief stated that presidents should not be subject to criminal proceedings and that the only legal

SUPREME COURT PROCEEDINGS

For each case, Supreme Court justices look at records from previous court proceedings and decisions, as well as a legal brief submitted by each side that covers the arguments, precedents, and legal issues. Each side is permitted 30 minutes to present the case and answer questions by the justices. Because each case has already been through trial, no additional witnesses are called. The justices then meet to discuss the case they have heard and vote on it. Oral arguments are open to the public, although seating is limited.

recourse for a sitting president, short of challenging him in an election, was impeachment.

Jaworski's Legal Brief

In his own brief, Jaworski argued that the case was focused solely on the issue of whether the president had to honor the subpoena in the current circumstances. Jaworski claimed the court's decision would not have far-ranging effects on the relationships between the branches of government. He countered St. Clair's argument that the Supreme Court did not have jurisdiction to decide a dispute between members of the executive branch by stating that one of the fundamental functions of the court is to act as a neutral branch of government, resolving issues of conflict or controversy based on the law. In this case, the Justice Department was trying a criminal case, for which it needed evidence, and the president was opposing that quest for evidence based on a claim of executive privilege. Jaworski said the court had every right to settle such a dispute.

The brief went on to address the issue of executive privilege. Jaworski pointed out the conflict of interest occurring when a president is allowed to decide for

THE ROAD MAP

The special prosecutor's office had compiled a report containing the evidence concerning the president's involvement in Watergate to submit to the House Judiciary Committee for use in the impeachment proceedings. Jaworski's team was careful to include the facts of the case but to let the House Judiciary Committee draw its own conclusions, calling the document a "road map."[7] It was delivered in a sealed case to Judge Sirica for transmission to the committee. Haldeman contested the report's delivery to the House, arguing that publicity about the evidence could prevent a fair trial for him. Sirica ruled in favor of turning over the report, a decision that was upheld by the US court of appeals.

himself what evidence to turn over when the evidence in question might implicate him. Jaworski's brief argued,

> The President cannot be a proper judge of whether the greater public interest lies in disclosing evidence subpoenaed for trial, when that evidence may have a material bearing on whether he is impeached and will bear heavily on the guilt or innocence of close aides and trusted advisers.[6]

Jaworski's brief also asserted that the lack of mention of executive privilege in the Constitution

indicated the constitutional framers deliberately did not grant the president an explicit executive privilege.

If the president does have a limited executive privilege, it should only be used to protect the workings of the executive branch and not to protect evidence of criminal wrongdoing, the brief argued. As to whether the prosecution had demonstrated a compelling need to override the executive privilege, the brief explained why each specific recording was being requested and what evidence indicated each recording would be relevant to the criminal case. Finally, since the president had already allowed participants in the recorded conversations to speak about their content, he had weakened his argument for why they should continue to be protected. Jaworski argued,

> *The unusual circumstances of this case— where high government officials are under indictment for conspiracy to defraud the United States and obstruct justice—at once makes it imperative that the trial be conducted on the basis of all relevant evidence and at the same time make it highly unlikely that there will soon be a similar occasion to intrude on the confidentiality of the Executive Branch.*[8]

The Judges

The Supreme Court justices reviewed the briefs in preparation for hearing **oral arguments** and researched the constitutional questions in preparation for the hearing. While the Supreme Court consists of nine justices, only eight would hear *The United States v. Nixon*. If a judge has a potential conflict of interest in a case, he or she can decline to participate in the proceedings, which is called a recusal. Because Justice William Rehnquist had a personal connection to several parties in the Watergate case, he recused himself from the decision on the petition for the writ of certiorari, as well as from the *The United States v. Nixon* case. With an even number of justices, the vote could result in a tie, in which case the court would uphold Judge Sirica's decision on the subpoenas. However, the president had said he would abide by a definitive decision by the Supreme Court. Jaworski later noted,

> *I had reason to believe now that if the vote against [Nixon] was close he would go on television and tell the people that the presidency should not be impaired by a divided Court.*[9]

oral argument—A spoken presentation of a legal case by a lawyer.

Chief Justice Warren Burger, *front center*, poses with the other eight justices at the time of *The United States v. Nixon*. William Rehnquist, *top right*, recused himself from the case.

Of the eight justices who would hear the case, three had been appointed by Nixon himself. During his 1968 presidential campaign, one of Nixon's campaign promises was to make conservative judicial appointments and select judges who would be tough on criminals and serve the needs of law enforcement agencies.

President Eisenhower had appointed Chief Justice Warren Burger to the US Court of Appeals for the

District of Columbia in 1955. In 1969, Nixon named Burger to the Supreme Court to replace Chief Justice Earl Warren. Nixon also appointed Associate Justices Lewis Powell and Harry Blackmun. Eisenhower appointed William Brennan in 1956 and Potter Stewart in 1958. Brennan was known as a liberal constructionist, meaning he did not abide by a strict interpretation of the Constitution.

Previous Democratic presidents had appointed three of the justices. Franklin Roosevelt appointed William Douglas, the most senior member of the court, in 1939. Byron White was a Kennedy appointee, named to the court in 1962. White tended to vote with the moderate or conservative justices. President Lyndon B. Johnson appointed Thurgood Marshall, the country's first African-American Supreme Court justice, in 1967.

With five of the eight voting justices having been appointed during either Nixon's presidency or vice presidency, and a sixth justice who sometimes voted with the conservative justices, at first glance the court appeared to be weighted in the president's favor. But they had yet to hear oral arguments and debate one of the most crucial cases in US history. ∽

Chapter 8

The Hearing

*T*he oral arguments for *The United States v. Nixon* began on July 8, 1974. In most cases, the Supreme Court allows each side 30 minutes for oral argument. In the case of *Nixon*, however, each side was permitted a total of 90 minutes. Jaworski was given 60 minutes to present his case, followed by 75 minutes for St. Clair to present his argument. Philip Lacovara, counsel to the special prosecutor, had 30 minutes for rebuttal, and then St. Clair had 15 more minutes to close.

During Jaworski's hour-long presentation, the justices stopped him 115 times to ask for clarifications or explanations of the legal points. Several of the justices had questions about how Nixon's status as an unindicted coconspirator was

St. Clair defends Nixon before the Supreme Court.

relevant to the issue of the evidence. Jaworski spoke to how the president's status made such evidence admissible to trial. However, his main point was about the judicial branch's important role in interpreting the Constitution, and the dangers of letting a president single-handedly decide what he can do. Jaworski argued,

> *This nation's constitutional form of government is in serious jeopardy if the President, any President, is to say that the Constitution means what he says it does, and that there is no one, not even the Supreme Court, to tell him otherwise.*[1]

St. Clair argued the opposite, that the Supreme Court had no say in proceedings that were rightfully the domain of the executive branch. Justice Powell asked him, "What public interest is there in preserving secrecy with respect to a criminal conspiracy?" St. Clair responded: "The answer, sir, is that a criminal conspiracy is criminal only after it's proven to be criminal."[2]

In his rebuttal, Lacovara refuted St. Clair's argument that the criminal trial for which the evidence had been subpoenaed was linked to the House Judiciary Committee's impeachment inquiry. Jaworski remembered feeling confident as he left the courtroom. At one point, Justice Douglas had asked, "Well, we start with a Constitution that does not contain the words

'executive privilege'—is that right?" "That is right, sir," Jaworski had responded.[3]

The Opinion

Although the justices disagreed while debating the issue in chambers, they felt it was important to reach a unanimous decision because of Nixon's statement that he would abide by a definitive ruling. They believed there was a chance Nixon would not heed their opinion if the court was divided or if the opinion was not strongly worded. Chief Justice Burger assigned himself to write the opinion, but the other justices suggested major revisions to his first draft. Many of their ideas were incorporated, and Justice Stewart ultimately coauthored the opinion with Burger. The final draft worked toward settling the specific issue before the court regarding the

AT THE HEARING

Oral arguments for Supreme Court cases are open to the public, but the small amount of seating is available on a first-come, first-served basis. At *The United States v. Nixon* hearing some seats were reserved for reporters, lawyers, and members of Congress. Some members of the public camped with sleeping bags outside the Supreme Court for two nights in an attempt to get seats to this important case.

subpoenaed tapes as well as establishing a constitutional
doctrine for executive privilege.

The Supreme Court delivered its opinion on
July 24, the same day the House Judiciary Committee's
public hearings were set to start. The court had voted
unanimously in favor of upholding Judge Sirica's
decision on the subpoenas. President Nixon would be
required to turn over the subpoenaed materials.

Chief Justice Burger read the opinion aloud to a
packed court. First, he addressed the issue of whether the
court had jurisdiction to hear the case. The justices had

judicial review—The power of a court to examine an executive or
legislative act and to refute the act if it is unconstitutional.

110

Chief Justice Burger read the court's opinion, which ruled against Nixon.

decided the facts of the case warranted **judicial review**. The opinion noted that the special prosecutor had the specific authority to challenge executive privilege, and therefore had **standing to sue** the president despite being his subordinate. On the issue of separation of powers and the judicial branch's interference in the workings of the executive or legislative branches, Burger quoted the opinion from *Marbury v. Madison*: "It is emphatically the province and the duty of the judicial department to say what the law is."[5]

Burger next spoke to St. Clair's contention that the subpoenaed tapes did not meet the requirements for subpoenaed materials. To be subpoenaed, materials need to be relevant, unattainable through other reasonable means, necessary for trial preparations, and admissible during trial. The Supreme Court determined the special prosecutor had met these requirements.

The chief justice went on to deliver the Supreme Court's first definitive stance on the issue of executive privilege:

standing to sue—The requirement in law that the party bringing legal action against another party has the right to bring the lawsuit and has a personal stake in the outcome of the legal action.

Neither the doctrine of separation of powers nor the need for confidentiality of high level communications . . . can sustain an absolute, unqualified presidential privilege of immunity from judicial process under all circumstances.[6]

The opinion described limited circumstances in which an executive privilege could be recognized, including in matters related to military, diplomatic, or national security issues. It also recognized the president's need to speak candidly with his staff and stated that while the Constitution does not explicitly guarantee confidentiality, a reasonable expectation of it is necessary for the president to carry out his presidential duties.

St. Clair had argued that the executive privilege was absolute, which would have meant the president could decide to exercise it

> "The President wants me to argue that he is as powerful a monarch as Louis XIV, only four years at a time, and is not subject to the processes of any court in the land except the court of impeachment."[7]
>
> —*JAMES ST. CLAIR, ATTORNEY FOR RICHARD NIXON*

in any circumstances on his own behalf. However, the court found the privilege to be not absolute and that

it should be weighed against other matters of public interest. An absolute privilege would interfere with the judicial branch's constitutional obligations to conduct criminal prosecutions in a fair and just manner. In this case, the court had to balance the president's need for free and private communication with his staff against the court system's need to obtain evidence for criminal prosecutions. The court determined that in this case, the president was relying on a general presumption of executive privilege and did not have a specific compelling reason—such as national security—to keep the subpoenaed tapes private. It acknowledged that criminal cases requiring access to the president's private conversations were unlikely to happen frequently, and

CRITICISMS OF THE OPINION

Author James Doyle summarized some of the eventual criticisms scholars had of the Supreme Court opinion in his book *Not Above the Law*:

> It was overly broad, they would say; it invoked John Marshall's sweeping [opinion] without distinction or reservation; it failed to mention the specific evidence of criminality in this case which might have helped draw a narrower ruling; it accepted executive privilege without adequately discussing its justification.[8]

therefore upholding the subpoenas was not likely to impede future presidents' communications with their advisers. The opinion concluded that the requirements of due process in the pending criminal case overrode the president's claim of executive privilege. "The generalized assertion of privilege must yield to the demonstrated, specific need for evidence in a pending criminal trial."[9]

With its unanimous decision, the court ordered Nixon to turn over the 64 tapes requested by the special prosecutor. ~

Chapter 9

The Fallout

When he was informed of the unanimous Supreme Court decision, President Nixon expressed shock that his own Supreme Court appointees had not supported him. He and his advisers spent hours deciding on a response. One option he considered was destroying the tapes and resigning from the presidency immediately. One of his advisers suggested Nixon continue refusing to turn over the tapes on the principle of protecting presidential power. However, St. Clair concluded from the Supreme Court decision that the president had no room to defy the court. He urged Nixon to comply unconditionally with the subpoena. St. Clair and Haig told the president anything less would certainly lead to his impeachment. At the end of the day,

The Supreme Court's ruling upheld the subpoena and required Nixon to turn over the requested tapes to the prosecution.

Nixon made a statement, telling Americans, "I respect and accept the Court's decision."[1] However, St. Clair told the press that reviewing the tapes and complying with the subpoena could take several weeks. Jaworski and St. Clair met with Judge Sirica to set a timetable for the turnover of the tapes to the prosecution.

Meanwhile, the House Judiciary Committee had begun public hearings in the impeachment trial on July 24. Within a week of the hearings' beginnings, it had approved three articles of impeachment: obstruction of justice, abuse of power, and contempt of Congress. In each case, all 21 Democrats on the committee voted in favor of the article, with a varying number of Republicans joining them.

On August 5, the tape of the June 23, 1972, meeting between Nixon and Haldeman was turned over to the prosecution. While many of the other tapes contained evidence of criminal wrongdoing, this tape was considered to be the smoking gun. The tape clearly showed that Nixon was aware of the circumstances of the Watergate burglary and the ensuing cover-up five days after it occurred. This contradicted Nixon's lawyers' statements that the president had not known about the cover-up until March 1973. On the tape,

TRANSCRIPTS VS. TAPES

While quarreling over the subpoenas, the president's lawyers and the special prosecutor had disagreed whether edited transcripts would suffice or if the president needed to turn over the actual recordings. When the tapes were released, glaring differences were apparent between the true dialogue and the edited transcripts made available earlier in the legal process. The transcript for one exchange from a meeting between Nixon and Ehrlichman that occurred on April 14, 1973, merely reads: "material unrelated to presidential action."[2] On the tape, Nixon can be heard saying, "And before I leave office and they'll get off. You get them full pardons. That's what they have to have, John."[3]

Haldeman listed participants in the crime, and Nixon instructed him on how to cover up what had happened. The two men discussed having the CIA interfere in the FBI investigation and how they could say national security was the reason for the interference. The tape proved Nixon was actively trying to interfere in the Watergate investigation.

Upon hearing the tape, the Republican members of the House Judiciary Committee who had previously voted against the articles of impeachment changed their votes. The impeachment trial of Nixon would soon begin in the Senate. It became clear Nixon's presidency

On August 8, 1974, Nixon became the first president to resign from office; as of 2012, he was the only president to have done so.

would not survive the impeachment trial. It was estimated that Nixon could count on the support of no more than 12 to 15 senators, not nearly enough to keep him in office. On August 8, 1974, Nixon resigned from the presidency. In his televised speech, he did not admit criminal wrongdoing. Instead he claimed he was resigning because "I no longer have a strong enough political base in Congress."[4]

"Our long national nightmare is over," declared former vice president Ford when he was sworn in as the new president. "Our Constitution works; our great Republic is a government of laws and not of men."[5]

Whether to Prosecute

The issue of the tapes behind them, Jaworski and his team now considered whether to prosecute the former president. He had been named as an unindicted coconspirator because Jaworski had not wanted to prosecute a sitting president during an impeachment trial. But now Nixon had stepped down, and there was enough evidence to indict and prosecute him. Most of Jaworski's staff supported prosecution, but he had doubts. For one thing, he felt the impeachment inquiry and resignation had already settled the matter. Making

the former president the defendant in a criminal trial would be hard on the country, and publicity surrounding Watergate might impede a fair trial. On the other hand, many on Jaworski's staff felt justice should be carried out equally, and Nixon should face the same fate as the aides who had carried out his wishes. According to the Constitution, the former president could be tried in court following an impeachment hearing.

One of the lawyers working for Jaworski, Richard Davis, wrote a memo summarizing the issues. Davis referred to other cases in which a prosecution or investigation had been abandoned because it had not been in the public's interest to pursue it. But he went on to point out the potential for injustice in applying the laws differently to different people if Nixon should go free while Haldeman and the numerous others involved in Watergate were tried and sentenced. Davis wrote,

> *Our history is unfortunately filled with instances of justice being applied with an uneven hand [but] it is rare indeed that one decision has the potential to so boldly demonstrate the unfair and unequal manner in which our system of justice can operate.*[6]

Lacovara, counsel for the special prosecutor, pointed out it was unlikely Nixon would serve a prison sentence.

Even if he were sentenced to serve time, the attorney general would be able to designate an alternative location for confinement. Lacovara further contended that Nixon had still not accepted responsibility for criminal wrongdoing and intended to continue participating in public life. Since the impeachment trial had been cut short, no findings had been made of the president's guilt or innocence. Furthermore, Lacovara did not believe Nixon's resignation was a sufficient punishment for his crimes. "The office was not 'his' but was a public trust that he violated and forfeited."[8]

IMPEACHMENT AND PROSECUTION

Article 1, Section 3 of the US Constitution states:

> Judgment in Cases of Impeachment shall not extend further than to removal from Office, and disqualification to hold and enjoy any Office of honor, Trust or Profit under the United States: but the Party convicted shall nevertheless be liable and subject to Indictment, Trial, Judgment and Punishment, according to Law.[7]

Nixon's impeachment could only remove him from office, not indict or convict him of the crimes for which he was impeached. However, after his impeachment trial he could be indicted for the same crimes in a separate trial.

Jaworski's primary concern was whether the president could receive a fair trial, a right guaranteed in the Constitution. In criminal law, a defendant is presumed innocent until proven guilty. However, many people had already assumed Nixon's guilt due to the televised impeachment hearings, media coverage, and the president's resignation. A jury is supposed to base its decision only on evidence it hears during the trial, not on information received outside the trial, and this would have been difficult to achieve in Nixon's case. Jaworski did not want to indict Nixon unless he could reasonably expect to try him. Herbert Miller, an attorney for Nixon, wrote to Jaworski expressing similar concerns about the unlikelihood of a fair trial. Jaworski concluded that if the court asked him if Nixon could receive a fair trial,

> " I brought myself down. I gave them a sword and they stuck it in. And I guess if I had been in their position, I would have done the same thing."[9]
> —RICHARD NIXON, 1977

he would have to answer no. He also did not know how much time would have to pass before the president could receive a fair trial.

WATERGATE CONVICTIONS

Some of those in favor of indicting Nixon argued he should be treated in the same way as those subordinates who were indicted and convicted for following his orders. The work of the special prosecutor's task force led to many convictions of high-level officials. Among them were:

- Charles Colson, counsel to the president: guilty of obstruction of justice, 1 to 3 years in prison.

- John Dean, counsel to the president: guilty of conspiracy to obstruct justice, 1 to 4 years in prison.

- H. R. Haldeman, White House chief of staff: guilty of conspiracy to obstruct justice, obstruction of justice, perjury, 2.5 to 8 years in prison.

- Jeb Magruder, White House and campaign aide: guilty of conspiracy to wiretap and conspiracy to obstruct justice, 10 months to 4 years in prison.

- John Mitchell, attorney general: guilty of conspiracy to obstruct justice, obstruction of justice, perjury, making false statements to the FBI, 2.5 to 8 years in prison.

Meanwhile, President Ford was considering the question of whether to pardon his predecessor. Jaworski did not want to indict Nixon only to have him pardoned, so he encouraged the White House to decide on a course of action before he took any action pertaining to an indictment. Soon the issue was taken

On September 8, Ford granted Nixon a full presidential pardon, freeing him from all criminal charges.

out of the prosecutor's hands. Ford granted Nixon a presidential pardon on September 8, 1974, ending any possibility that he would be tried for crimes related to

Watergate. Ford explained his decision, expressing his doubts that Nixon could receive a fair trial and his belief that the former president had suffered enough for his crimes. It was an unpopular decision; afterward, Ford's approval rating dropped from 71 to 49 percent.[10] ～

Chapter 10

Lasting Impact

*T*he *United States v. Nixon* is considered the landmark Supreme Court case on executive privilege. Presidents had been regularly asserting a right to an executive privilege since Washington was president. But it was not until the *Nixon* case that a clear constitutional basis was set forth for the privilege. The Supreme Court's unanimous decision set a legal precedent for cases decided since then. The court ruled against Nixon and rejected his claim of an absolute executive privilege that would have applied to all presidential records. However, at the same time, the justices recognized a limited executive privilege, and the court established its own role as the monitor of when the president's need to exercise

privilege outweighs someone else's need to override that privilege.

Since *The United States v. Nixon*, the Supreme Court has evaluated challenges of executive privilege on a case-by-case basis. The justices have to weigh several factors, as they did in the *Nixon* case. That case established executive privilege as strongest when exercised in areas pertaining to national security or military operations, but the privilege has also sometimes been upheld in cases regarding discussions that are clearly official government business. The court is most likely to override executive privilege in criminal cases.

CHANGES TO RECORD KEEPING

Since Nixon's use of recording devices ended up being used against him, presidents no longer record conversations. Presidents and their staffs also have become more reluctant to keep detailed written records, including meeting notes, personal diaries, and e-mails. As a result of this shift, historians no longer have the detailed records of the inner workings of the executive branch such as those created before Watergate. "The price of Nixon's indiscretions will be paid by generations of scholars who will be deprived of an extraordinarily rich resource," wrote one political scientist.[1]

The Fate of Presidential Records

Nixon himself put the privilege to the test again after leaving office. Following his resignation, Nixon attempted to keep control of his personal papers and records as past presidents had done. He expected to need them to fulfill further subpoenas, as well as to consult while writing his memoirs. Ford's staff halted the shipment of the records to Nixon's home in California. A compromise was reached in which Nixon retained ownership of his documents but they were deposited in the National Archives in Washington DC rather than in Nixon's home. Jaworski opposed the agreement due to the ongoing criminal investigation of Nixon's staff. In response, Congress passed the Presidential Recordings and Materials Preservation Act of 1974, which gave control of Nixon's presidential records to the National Archives.

Nixon sued in court for control of his tapes and documents, asserting that the new law violated his rights. According to his legal team, the law violated executive privilege, separation of powers, right to privacy, freedom of expression, protection against unlawful search and

majority opinion—An explanation of the reasoning behind the majority decision of the Supreme Court.

Today, Nixon's papers can be seen at the Nixon Presidential Library in Yorba Linda, California.

seizure, and equal treatment under the law. The case went before the Supreme Court in 1977. By a margin of 7–2, the justices upheld the law. In the **majority opinion**, Justice Brennan argued that the public interest in retaining presidential records outweighed violations of Nixon's individual rights. The majority of the court had determined a president's claim to executive privilege

was not as strong after he left office as when in office, and the records needed to be preserved for legal and historical purposes. Burger and Rehnquist dissented, arguing the decision would impede future presidents' open communication with executive staff members.

Congress passed a new law in 1978, making most presidential records public property after a president leaves office. Materials of a sensitive nature would be released 12 years after the end of the presidential term. Nixon continued to fight against the release of the materials, but beginning in 1987 they were made public.

Other Presidents and Privilege

In light of what happened during the Nixon presidency, presidents Ford and Jimmy Carter did not make overt claims of executive privilege. But later presidents Ronald Reagan, George H. W. Bush, and Bill Clinton asserted it on numerous occasions. Many times these claims went unchallenged or were addressed through political means. Occasionally the question of privilege ended up back in court. During Clinton's presidency, former Arkansas state employee Paula Jones sued Clinton, accusing him of sexual harassment during the time he was governor of Arkansas. In 1997, Clinton's lawyers

CLINTON'S PRIVILEGE

Journalists and legal experts debated Bill Clinton's 1998 assertion of executive privilege. One journalist compared the situation to Nixon's case:

> Not since Richard Nixon tried to withhold incriminating taped evidence—and was forced by the unanimous Supreme Court to respond to the subpoena of a grand jury—has a president presumed to wrap personal wrongdoing in the cloak of official business.[2]

Other journalists disagreed, arguing Clinton's case was different from Nixon's. In *The United States v. Nixon*, the prosecutor had produced evidence constituting probable cause that the subpoenaed tapes were crucial to the investigation. In the journalist's opinion, prosecutor Kenneth Starr had not satisfied probable cause for overriding executive privilege.

argued a civil suit could not be brought against a sitting president, but the Supreme Court unanimously rejected this claim. It decided that while presidents could not be sued for official acts, they could be brought to court on misconduct committed prior to becoming a president.

Clinton attempted to claim executive privilege in 1998, when he objected to the questioning of two of his aides during the investigation of an alleged affair between Clinton and White House intern Monica

Like Nixon, President Clinton underwent an impeachment trial, although he was acquitted.

Lewinsky. He argued such conversations should remain confidential to protect the president's ability to converse freely with his advisers. "One cannot overstate the intolerable threat that an unduly constrictive reading of the privilege poses to the President's ability to get frank

and candid advice from his advisers," his lawyers argued.[3] However, in Clinton's case, neither the conversations nor the behavior in question concerned official government matters. The courts rejected Clinton's claims of privilege, relying largely on the precedent set by *The United States v. Nixon*.

President George W. Bush and Vice President Richard Cheney for the most part handled within the executive branch questions of when to apply executive privilege and what information would be released outside of the courts. One case made it to the Supreme Court during Bush's eight-year tenure as president. Environmental activists had alleged that lobbyists and executives from the oil and gas industry were being allowed to attend closed-door meetings with Cheney

BUSH AND NIXON

Some commentators compared the tendencies toward secrecy during the administration of George W. Bush to those of the Nixon administration. John Dean, the White House counsel who was indicted for the Watergate cover-up, published a book in 2004 called *Worse than Watergate*, in which he criticized the lack of transparency in the Bush White House. He listed many examples, but in particular focused on the argument Bush made to Congress and the public in support of the Iraq War.

regarding energy policy, which was in possible violation of open-meeting laws. They filed suit against Cheney to obtain the information. Bush's lawyers did not use the term executive privilege, but they claimed they did not have to release the requested information. The Supreme Court case was known as *Cheney v. United States District Court for D.C.* The Supreme Court decided 7–2 in favor of Bush and Cheney. The opinion cited a clear difference between this case and *The United States v. Nixon*: "The need for information for use in civil cases, while far from negligible, does not share the urgency or significance of the criminal subpoena requests in *Nixon*."[4]

Many times claims of executive privilege go unchallenged in court, depending on the circumstances surrounding the requested information and how likely it is the claim would be upheld based on existing case law. In cases in which Congress is conducting an investigation of someone in the executive branch, often the two branches will negotiate between themselves over the disclosure of information without involving the judicial branch.

Evolving Executive Power

While *The United States v. Nixon* provided a clearer picture of the circumstances in which presidents can expect to exercise executive privilege, some questions have remained unanswered. Based on the court opinion, it is uncertain how long presidential communications need to remain secret to respect a president's needs for candid discussion with his or her advisers. The court also left unclear whether a sitting president can choose to revoke the executive privilege of a former president, or

SPECIAL PROSECUTOR LAWS

The Ethics in Government Act has been modified several times over the years to address concerns about its cost and its purpose. Revisions changed the special prosecutor position's title to "independent counsel," gave more power to the attorney general regarding the position's appointment or removal, and limited who in the executive branch could be investigated.[5] The Reagan administration opposed the independent counsel position as unconstitutional because it created a position within the executive branch that was not controlled by the executive. Others thought independent counsel investigations would be used to unnecessarily harass officials. However, when the case reached the Supreme Court, the justices upheld the constitutionality of the law.

whether executive privilege can be used to enforce silence among the president's staff.

Watergate led to a variety of reforms meant to curb presidential power and ensure a scandal of similar proportion would not happen again. In 1978, Congress passed the Ethics in Government Act, which created financial disclosure requirements for elected officials. It also established procedures for appointing an independent counsel in the event an executive needed to be investigated again. The attorney general would determine if probable cause for an investigation existed, and then a three-judge panel would appoint an independent counsel if needed. The law also set limits on how an independent counsel could be removed. These new procedures were meant to address concerns that the special prosecutor had not been able to act independently during the investigation of Nixon.

> " Watergate transformed and reshaped American attitudes toward government, and especially the presidency, more than any single event since the Great Depression of the 1930s."[6]
>
> —STANLEY I. KUTLER, WATERGATE HISTORIAN

In the wake of Watergate, there was also a movement toward a more open, transparent government. The Freedom of Information Act had been passed in 1966 to improve access to information about government activities, but Congress scrutinized the issue again following Nixon's resignation. Changes to the law set stricter time limits for fulfilling requests and provided guidelines for judicial review.

Not all of these reforms lasted, but the Watergate scandal and the *The United States v. Nixon* decision have had a lasting effect on the nature of presidential power. Nixon had tried unsuccessfully to cast the office of the president as infallible and all-powerful. But the highest court found that he was not above the law and that the public's interest in carrying out justice outweighed the president's interest in confidentiality. The carefully worded opinion carved out a limited executive privilege that has been used as a road map of the issue ever since. ～

TIMELINE OF EVENTS AND RULINGS

1968

November 5 — Richard Nixon is elected president of the United States.

1972

June 17 — Five men are arrested after breaking into the offices of the Democratic National Committee at the Watergate complex.

June 23 — Nixon and his chief of staff meet to discuss a cover-up for the Watergate burglaries, a conversation that becomes public more than two years later.

November 7 — Nixon is reelected in a landslide victory.

1973

January 30 — G. Gordon Liddy and James W. McCord Jr. are convicted of conspiracy, burglary, and wiretapping.

April 30 — Chief of Staff H. R. Haldeman, White House aide John Ehrlichman, and Attorney General Richard Kleindienst resign over the Watergate scandal.

May 17 — The Senate begins hearings on Watergate.

July 23 — Special Prosecutor Archibald Cox subpoenas a list of tapes pertaining to the investigation.

August 29 — Judge John Sirica upholds the subpoena and orders Nixon to make the tapes available.

October 12 — The Court of Appeals for the District of Columbia upholds Sirica's decision on the subpoena.

1973	**October 20**	Cox is fired in what becomes known as the Saturday Night Massacre.
1974	**January 30**	President Nixon delivers his State of the Union address, asserting he will turn over no more evidence pertaining to the Watergate investigation.
	April 18	Sirica grants a subpoena to the new special prosecutor, Leon Jaworski, for tapes and materials needed for the Watergate investigation.
	April 30	The White House releases more than 1,000 pages of edited transcripts of the tapes to the House Judiciary Committee.
	May 31	The Supreme Court grants the writ for certiorari for *The United States v. Nixon* instead of waiting for a decision from the court of appeals.
	July 8	The Supreme Court hears oral arguments in the case of *The United States v. Nixon.*
	July 24	The Supreme Court rules unanimously that Nixon must honor the subpoena, establishing a limited but not absolute basis for executive privilege.
	July 27	The House Judiciary Committee passes the first of three articles of impeachment, charging the president with obstruction of justice.
	August 8	Nixon becomes the first president in US history to resign, turning over the presidency to Gerald Ford.
	September 8	President Gerald Ford pardons Nixon for crimes related to Watergate.

GLOSSARY

common law
> A body or system of law based on reason and general custom; applied to situations not covered by legislation.

Communist
> A believer in a theory that advocates for shared wealth and the elimination of private property and companies.

doctrine
> A principle of law established through past decisions.

implicate
> To connect an individual to a crime.

incumbent
> Someone who holds an office or position.

innuendo
> A hint or insinuation at something that is not stated clearly.

pardon
> To excuse someone from an offense without punishment.

partisan
> Expressing firm support for a party or person, especially prejudiced or unreasonable support.

rebuttal
> A response to a legal argument that aims to dispute the argument.

recuse

> To disqualify oneself from participation in something due to personal bias or a conflict of interest.

slush fund

> A reserve of money with little to no regulation that is often used for secret or illegal purposes.

smear campaign

> A campaign for elected office that portrays an opponent in a way that harms the opponent's reputation.

smoking gun

> A piece of evidence that provides conclusive proof of a suspect's guilt.

subordinate

> One who stands in order or rank below another.

tenure

> The amount of time a person owns or holds something, such as a position.

wiretapping

> The undisclosed monitoring of a private telephone conversation by a third party to gain information.

BRIEFS

Petitioner

The United States government

Respondent

President Richard Nixon

Date of Ruling

July 24, 1974

Summary of Impacts

After members of Nixon's staff were accused of breaking
into the Democratic National Committee headquarters at
the Watergate building, Nixon refused to honor a subpoena
requesting tapes featuring conversations between Nixon and
members of his staff. Nixon cited executive privilege, but the
special prosecutor believed the tapes would be the smoking gun
to implicate Nixon and high-ranking members of the executive
branch in the crime. The case made it to the US Supreme
Court in 1974. The Supreme Court ruled unanimously to
uphold the subpoena, deciding that in that case the public
need for specific evidence to prosecute a criminal trial of
high-ranking officials in the executive branch overrode the
president's claim to executive privilege. Following the ruling,
Nixon resigned from office. He was pardoned by his successor,
President Gerald Ford, in the fall of 1974.

    The United States v. Nixon was the Supreme Court's first
definitive ruling on the issue of executive privilege. It denied
President Nixon's claim and ruled that an absolute executive

privilege does not exist. However, it also recognized that a limited executive privilege does have a constitutional basis, because the president needs to be able to communicate freely with advisers to carry out the duties of the office. Privilege is given particular weight when matters of national security or military secrets are in question. However, in some instances privilege can be overridden when a matter of greater public interest is at stake.

Quote

"This nation's constitutional form of government is in serious jeopardy if the President, any President, is to say that the Constitution means what he says it does, and that there is no one, not even the Supreme Court, to tell him otherwise."

—Leon Jaworski, special prosecutor

ADDITIONAL RESOURCES

Selected Bibliography

Doyle, James. *Not Above the Law: The Battles of Watergate Prosecutors Cox and Jaworski.* New York: William Morrow, 1977. Print.

Jaworski, Leon. *The Right and the Power: The Prosecution of Watergate.* New York: Reader's Digest, 1976. Print.

Kutler, Stanley I. *The Wars of Watergate: The Last Crisis of Richard Nixon.* New York: Norton, 1990. Print.

Savage, David G. *The Supreme Court and the Powers of the American Government.* Washington DC: CQ, 2009. Print.

Small, Melvin. *The Presidency of Richard Nixon.* Lawrence, KS: UP of Kansas, 1999. Print.

Further Readings

Panchyk, Richard. *Our Supreme Court: A History with 14 Activities.* Chicago: Chicago Review, 2006. Print.

Pederson, Charles E. *The U.S. Constitution and the Bill of Rights.* Edina, MN: Abdo, 2010. Print.

Web Links

To learn more about *The United States v. Nixon*, visit ABDO Publishing Company online at **www.abdopublishing.com**. Web sites about *Nixon* are featured on our Book Links page. These links are routinely monitored and updated to provide the most current information available.

Places to Visit

Nixon Presidential Library and Museum

18001 Yorba Linda Boulevard, Yorba Linda, CA 92886
714-983-9120
http://www.nixonlibrary.gov
This museum houses the presidential materials from the Nixon administration, including texts, photographs, and tapes.

US Supreme Court

1 First Street, NE, Washington, DC
202-479-3000
http://www.supremecourt.gov
Visitors to the Supreme Court can take a self-guided tour or attend oral arguments if a case is being heard. The building is open to visitors Monday through Friday from 9 a.m. to 4:30 p.m.

SOURCE NOTES

Chapter 1. Straight to the Supreme Court

1. Leon Jaworski. *The Right and the Power: The Prosecution of Watergate.* New York: Reader's Digest, 1976. Print. 89.

2. Ibid. 92.

3. Ibid. 148.

4. "Rule 20. Procedure on a Petition for an Extraordinary Writ." *Supreme Court Rules.* Cornell University Law School, n.d. Web. 10 Aug. 2011.

5. Leon Jaworski. *The Right and the Power: The Prosecution of Watergate.* New York: Reader's Digest, 1976. Print. 162–163.

6. Leon Friedman and William F. Levantrosser. *Watergate and Afterward: The Legacy of Richard M. Nixon.* Westport, CT: Greenwood, 1992. Print. 106.

7. Melvin Small. *The Presidency of Richard Nixon.* Lawrence, KS: UP of Kansas, 1999. Print. 273.

Chapter 2. The Historical Roots of Executive Privilege

1. David G. Savage. *The Supreme Court and the Powers of the American Government.* Washington DC: CQ, 2009. Print. 328.

2. Michael G. Trachtman. *The Supremes' Greatest Hits: The 34 Supreme Court Cases That Most Directly Affect Your Life.* New York: Sterling, 2006. Print. 120.

3. Ibid. 25

4. "Constitution of the United States: A Transcription." *The Charters of Freedom.* National Archives and Records Administration, n.d. Web. 5 July 2011.

5. Michael G. Trachtman. *The Supremes' Greatest Hits: The 34 Supreme Court Cases That Most Directly Affect Your Life.* New York: Sterling, 2006. Print. 27.

6. David G. Savage. *The Supreme Court and the Powers of the American Government.* Washington DC: CQ, 2009. Print. 328.

7. Ibid. 213.

8. Michael G. Trachtman. *The Supremes' Greatest Hits: The 34 Supreme Court Cases That Most Directly Affect Your Life.* New York: Sterling, 2006. Print. 20.

9. David G. Savage. *The Supreme Court and the Powers of the American Government.* Washington DC: CQ, 2009. Print. 329.

Chapter 3. The Rise of Richard Nixon

1. Stanley I. Kutler. *The Wars of Watergate: The Last Crisis of Richard Nixon.* New York: W. W. Norton, 1990. Print. 34.

2. Ibid. 43.

3. Stanley I. Kutler. *The Wars of Watergate: The Last Crisis of Richard Nixon.* New York: W. W. Norton, 1990. Print. 45.

4. "Richard M. Nixon: 'Checkers.'" *American Rhetoric.* American Rhetoric, n.d. Web. 14 Mar. 2012.

5. "Richard M. Nixon." *Encyclopædia Britannica.* Encyclopædia Britannica, 2011. Web. 2 Mar. 2011.

6. Ibid.

7. Stanley I. Kutler. *The Wars of Watergate: The Last Crisis of Richard Nixon.* New York: W. W. Norton, 1990. Print. 71.

8. Ibid. 81.

9. Stanley I. Kutler. *The Wars of Watergate: The Last Crisis of Richard Nixon.* New York: W. W. Norton, 1990. Print. 81.

10. David G. Savage. *The Supreme Court and the Powers of the American Government.* Washington DC: CQ, 2009. Print. 330.

11. Ibid. 330.

12. Stanley I. Kutler. The Wars of Watergate: The Last Crisis of Richard Nixon. New York: W. W. Norton, 1990. Print. 109.

Chapter 4. Watergate Erupts

1. Melvin Small. *The Presidency of Richard Nixon.* Lawrence, KS: UP of Kansas, 1999. Print. 256.

2. Ibid. 263.

3. Stanley I. Kutler. *The Wars of Watergate: The Last Crisis of Richard Nixon.* New York: W. W. Norton, 1990. Print. 254.

4. Melvin Small. *The Presidency of Richard Nixon.* Lawrence, KS: UP of Kansas, 1999. Print. 281.

5. Ibid. 281.

6. "Editorial: Watergate: The Unfinished Business." *Washington Post.* Washington Post Company, 1 May 1973. Web. 6 Aug. 2011.

7. James Doyle. *Not Above the Law: The Battles of Watergate Prosecutors Cox and Jaworski.* New York: William Morrow, 1977. Print. 37.

8. Ibid. 40.

SOURCE NOTES CONTINUED

9. Ibid. 44.
10. Ibid. 47.

Chapter 5. The Investigation

1. Melvin Small. *The Presidency of Richard Nixon*. Lawrence, KS: UP of Kansas, 1999. Print. 283.
2. Ibid. 285.
3. Ibid. 285.
4. James Doyle. *Not Above the Law: The Battles of Watergate Prosecutors Cox and Jaworski*. New York: William Morrow, 1977. Print. 102.
5. Ibid. 105.
6. Ibid. 105.
7. Ibid. 112.
8. Bart Barnes. "John Sirica, Watergate judge, dies." *Washington Post*. Washington Post Company, 15 Aug. 1992. Web. 10 Aug. 2011.
9. James Doyle. *Not Above the Law: The Battles of Watergate Prosecutors Cox and Jaworski*. New York: William Morrow, 1977. Print. 118.
10. Ibid. 119.

Chapter 6. Subpoenas and Showdowns

1. James Doyle. *Not Above the Law: The Battles of Watergate Prosecutors Cox and Jaworski*. New York: William Morrow, 1977. Print. 185.
2. Ibid. 185.
3. Melvin Small. *The Presidency of Richard Nixon*. Lawrence, KS: UP of Kansas, 1999. Print. 290.
4. Leon Jaworski. *The Right and the Power: The Prosecution of Watergate*. New York: Reader's Digest, 1976. Print. 6.
5. Ibid. 36.
6. Ibid. 23.
7. Ibid. 75–76.
8. Ibid. 100.
9. Melvin Small. *The Presidency of Richard Nixon*. Lawrence, KS: UP of Kansas, 1999. Print. 292.

Chapter 7. The Supreme Court

1. "Due Process." *Legal Information Institute.* Cornell University Law School, n.d. Web. 10 Aug. 2011.

2. Robert Pear. "James St. Clair, Nixon's Watergate Lawyer, is Dead at 80." *New York Times.* New York Times Company, 12 Mar. 2001. Web. 1 Aug. 2011.

3. Leon Jaworski. *The Right and the Power: The Prosecution of Watergate.* New York: Reader's Digest, 1976. Print. 167.

4. Ibid. 168.

5. Ibid. 169.

6. Ibid. 172.

7. Ibid. 104.

8. Ibid. 174.

9. Ibid. 164.

Chapter 8. The Hearing

1. Leon Jaworski. *The Right and the Power: The Prosecution of Watergate.* New York: Reader's Digest, 1976. Print. 194.

2. James Doyle. *Not Above the Law: The Battles of Watergate Prosecutors Cox and Jaworski.* New York: William Morrow, 1977. Print. 333.

3. Leon Jaworski. *The Right and the Power: The Prosecution of Watergate.* New York: Reader's Digest, 1976. Print. 195–196.

4. Ibid. 192.

5. James Doyle. *Not Above the Law: The Battles of Watergate Prosecutors Cox and Jaworski.* New York: William Morrow, 1977. Print. 337.

6. David G. Savage. *The Supreme Court and the Powers of the American Government.* Washington DC: CQ, 2009. Print. 331.

7. Michael G. Trachtman. *The Supremes' Greatest Hits: The 34 Supreme Court Cases That Most Directly Affect Your Life.* New York: Sterling, 2006. Print. 131.

8. James Doyle. *Not Above the Law: The Battles of Watergate Prosecutors Cox and Jaworski.* New York: William Morrow, 1977. Print. 337.

9. David G. Savage. *The Supreme Court and the Powers of the American Government.* Washington DC: CQ, 2009. Print. 332.

Chapter 9. The Fallout

    1. Melvin Small. *The Presidency of Richard Nixon*. Lawrence, KS: UP of Kansas, 1999. Print. 293.

    2. Associate Press. "Nixon's Resignation Top Story of Year." *Observer-Reporter* 31 Dec. 1974. Google News, n. d. Web. 12 March 2012.

    3. Ibid.

    4. Melvin Small. *The Presidency of Richard Nixon*. Lawrence, KS: UP of Kansas, 1999. Print. 295.

    5. Michael G. Trachtman. *The Supremes' Greatest Hits: The 34 Supreme Court Cases That Most Directly Affect Your Life*. New York: Sterling, 2006. Print. 131.

    6. James Doyle. *Not Above the Law: The Battles of Watergate Prosecutors Cox and Jaworski*. New York: William Morrow, 1977. Print. 351.

    7. "The Charters of Freedom." *The Charters of Freedom*. National Archives, n. d. Web. 12 Mar. 2012.

    8. James Doyle. *Not Above the Law: The Battles of Watergate Prosecutors Cox and Jaworski*. New York: William Morrow, 1977. Print. 354.

    9. Robert A. Wilson, ed. *Power and the Presidency*. New York: PublicAffairs, 1999. Print. 109.

    10. Melvin Small. *The Presidency of Richard Nixon*. Lawrence, KS: UP of Kansas, 1999. Print. 300.

Chapter 10. Lasting Impact

1. Russell Riley. "The White House as a Black Box: Oral History and the Problem of Evidence in Presidential Studies." *Political Studies* 57.1. (2009): 187–206. Print. 194.

2. Jeffrey Rosen. "Underprivileged." *New Republic*. New Republic, 13 Apr. 1998. Web. 14 Mar. 2012.

3. Stephen Labaton. "President Decides to Abandon his Claim of Executive Privilege." *New York Times*. New York Times Company, 2 June 1998. Web. 10 Aug. 2011.

4. David G. Savage. *The Supreme Court and the Powers of the American Government*. Washington DC: CQ, 2009. Print. 334.

5. Stanley I. Kutler. *The Wars of Watergate: The Last Crisis of Richard Nixon*. New York: W. W. Norton, 1990. Print. 582–585.

6. Ibid. 607.

INDEX

A

Adams, John (counsel for the US army), 42
Agnew, Spiro, 44, 78–79
Army-McCarthy hearings, 42

B

Bernstein, Carl, 53, 94
Blackmun, Harry, 20–21, 105
Bork, Robert, 81
Brennan, William, 20, 105, 131–132
Brown v. Board of Education, 33
Burger, Warren, 21, 104–105, 109–110, 112, 132
Burr, Aaron, 31
Bush, George H. W., 132
Bush, George W., 135–136
Buzhardt, Fred, 71, 89
Byrd, Robert, 62–63

C

Carter, Jimmy, 132
Central Intelligence Agency, 52, 119
Chapin, Dwight, 51
Cheney, Richard, 135–136
Cheney v. United States District Court for D.C., 136
Chicago Southern Air Lines, Inc. v. Waterman Steamship Corporation, 33
Civil War, 32
Clinton, Bill, 132–135
Cold War, 38
Colson, Charles, 51, 58, 70, 125
Committee to Reelect the President, 51–53, 85
Communism, 38, 42
constitutional amendments
  Fifth, 95
  Fourteenth, 95
Cox, Archibald, 18, 60–63, 64, 66–69, 70–76, 78–79, 81, 83–85, 86, 89, 93

W

Y

About the Author

Erika Wittekind is a freelance writer and editor living in Wisconsin. She has a bachelor of arts degree in journalism and political science from Bradley University. She has covered education and government for several community newspapers, winning an award for best local news story from the Minnesota Newspapers Association for 2002. This is the fifth book she has written.

About the Content Consultant

Michael Gerhardt is Samuel Ashe Distinguished Professor of Constitutional Law at UNC-Chapel Hill. He is a nationally recognized expert on constitutional conflicts. He participated in the confirmation proceedings for five of the nine justices sitting on the Supreme Court in 2012. During President Clinton's impeachment proceedings, he testified as the only joint witness before the House of Representatives and served as CNN's full-time impeachment expert. He has published five books, including a leading treatise on the appointments process (published by Duke University Press) and *The Power of Precedent* (published by Oxford University Press). His forthcoming book, *The Constitutional Legacy of Forgotten Presidents*, will be published by Oxford University Press.